Forward

Based upon the successful Youtube accountancy videos this stu
with the definitive guide to the AAT Principles of Bookkeeping Controls unit. This book is written by a fellow of the Institute of Chartered Accountants of England and Wales who is a professional accountant of 29 years and current Finance Director.

Michael Norton is an expert in bookkeeping controls and able to bring this practical experience to teaching. The book explains not just the control but its objectives and then breaks down each exam question providing the most efficient technique to be applied and the traps set by the examiner that lead to failure.

The book is supported by an extensive library of videos and worked question examples from the author through YouTube, including walkthroughs of the AAT sample assessments, which can be found here:

Principles of Bookkeeping Controls - YouTube Michael Norton

The Principles of Bookkeeping controls unit is a short easy unit made long and difficult due to the approach many students or tutors adopt. Three key approaches used in this book that are different from the other methods /textbooks you may encounter. They are:

1) Each topic has a particular technique (control) to be applied. This will be the same for each question type regardless of the wording used;
2) The traps associated with the question type will be explained together with the question's required strategy;
3) Extensive question practice is provided. This book contains approximately 3 exam assessments (including a free assessment exam) worth of questions. Together with the AAT online practice exams (walkthroughs of the AAT assessment are provided in the playlist of videos) this is an extensive question bank.

Combined this provides comprehensive coverage of the exam syllabus.

Coupled with the YouTube videos this text will provide a less frustrating experience and more successful outcome. This book follows on from the Introduction to Bookkeeping unit and books which are also available on Amazon.

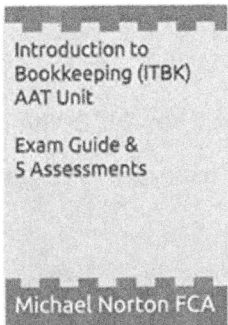

Contents

Forward 1

Introduction: How to Pass the Principles of Bookkeeping Controls Unit 4

Chapter 1 Recap of Introduction to Bookkeeping 7

    1.1 Debits and Credits 7

    1.2 T accounts 8

    1.3 VAT 10

    1.4 The Five Stage Accounting System 11

Chapter 2 What Is the Objective of Bookkeeping Controls? 16

Chapter 3 Payment Methods and Treasury Management 17

    3.1 Payment methods 17

    3.2 Treasury Management 23

Chapter 4 The Bank Statement and Bank Reconciliations 25

    4.1 The Importance of Cash 25

    4.2 Exam Technique 26

    4.3 The Four Steps of a Bank Reconciliation 27

    4.4 The Bank Statement 29

    4.5 Example of Bank Reconciliation 30

Chapter 5 Why Errors Occur –Classification of Errors and Impact Upon the Trial Balance 36

    5.1 Types of Error 36

        5.1.1 If the balance sheet balances why does it matter? 36

    5.2 Errors where the trial balance will still tally 37

        5.2.1 Error of Omission 37

        5.2.2 Error of Principle 37

        5.2.3 Error of Commission 38

        5.2.4 Error of Original Entry 38

        5.2.5 Error of reversal 38

        5.2.6 Compensating Error 39

    5.3 Errors that result in the trial balance not tallying 39

        5.3.1 Transposition Error and Different Credits and Debits 39

        5.3.2 Single Sided Errors or Two Errors on the Same Side of the Journal 39

        5.3.3 Miscasting error 39

        5.3.4 Extracting of Trial Balance Error 39

    5.4 Summary of Errors that affect and do not affect the trial balance 39

Chapter 6 Suspense Accounts and The Journal 42

    6.1 The Journal 45

Chapter 7 Trade Receivables and Trade Payables Control Account Reconciliations 48

7.1 Reconciliation of Trade Receivables Control Account and Sales Ledger 48

7.2 Reconciliation of Trade Payables Control Account and Purchases Ledger 51

7.3 Trade Receivables and Trade Payables Control T Account Questions 51

Chapter 8 The Journal and Postings to the Daybook 55

8.1 Opening balance when starting a company 56

8.2 Irrecoverable Debts 57

8.3 Suspense Accounts 58

8.3.1 Creation of a suspense account journal 58

8.3.2 Suspense T account 59

Chapter 9 VAT Control Account 63

9.1 Daybooks 63

9.2 The T Account 64

Chapter 10 Wages Control and Processing Wages Expenses 66

10.1 Wages Expenses 66

10.2 Paying the Wages Expense – the Wages Control 69

10.3 Control Accounts vs Suspense Accounts 72

Chapter 11 Extract and Initial Trial Balance and Update the Trial Balance - The Accounting Equation (Repeat from Introduction to Bookkeeping) 75

11.1 Balancing off an account 75

11.2 The Trial Balance 77

11.3 Creation of a Trial Balance 77

Chapter 12 Conclusion 81

Answers 82

Chapter 3 82

Chapter 4 82

Chapter 5 84

Chapter 6 85

Chapter 7 86

Chapter 8 87

Chapter 9 88

Chapter 10 90

Chapter 11 92

Index 94

Free practice assessment 96

Introduction: How to Pass the Principles of Bookkeeping Controls Unit

The Principles of Bookkeeping Controls unit should be undertaken over 50 guided learning hours and is one of the smaller units at level 2.

	Guided Learning Hours
Introduction to Bookkeeping	65
Principles of Bookkeeping Controls	50
Principles of Costing	50
The Business Environment	90

The learning outcomes only cover four distinct areas that will be tested in a 1.5 hour exam.

Learning outcomes	Weighting
1. Use control accounts	25%
2. Reconcile a bank statement with the cash book	25%
3. Use the journal	25%
4. Produce trial balances	25%
Total	100%

Despite being a small unit with limited requirements, this unit causes most problems for students at level 2. There are two reasons for this:

1) This unit requires a strong understanding of three parts of the Introduction to Bookkeeping unit, being:
    a. Double entry bookkeeping. In particular, understanding the cash movements behind debits and credits, T accounts and carried/brought down balances;
    b. Calculation of VAT; and
    c. The five stage accountancy system including daybooks, ledgers, supplier statements etc.

    Introduction to Bookkeeping **must** always be taken prior to this unit. It is possible to pass Introduction to Bookkeeping without the required knowledge for this unit through:

    i) Processing a number of financial documents; and
    ii) Using the DEAD CLIC approach for the opening trial balance. Unfortunately DEAD CLIC only explains what an account typically is (an asset being a debit a liability a credit etc.), not why a transaction is a debit (positive money) or credit (negative money) to the organisation (the account type plus whether it is increasing or decreasing).

    For this unit an understanding of why something has happened is required in order to produce the correct answer. This is because accounts will have transactions which increase and decrease the accounts balance (debits and credits in the same account) or include errors (requiring a reversal of the entry). The answer is often the reverse of DEAD CLIC.

It is also possible that the balance method of the accounting equation has been taught in the Introduction to Bookkeeping unit being:

$$\text{Assets - Liabilities = Capital}$$

Which is the statement of financial position for shareholders. This approach does not sufficiently explain the Business Entity concept of the Accounting Equation, which is that the owners of the company regardless of who they are (and including sole traders) are external to the company. Capital represents a money out item and a credit when increasing (with any reduction to capital owed, such as expenses, representing a debit). This understanding is more readily gained through the Accounting Equation being

Assets = Liabilities + Capital

Creating a clear T account of debits and credits on either side of the equation. T accounts feature heavily through the control account questions in this unit.

2) The questions in this unit can be broken down as follows:

Question	Approach	Requirement
Payments Methods	Memorise the different methods and timings of payments and apply to the scenario	Application of learnt knowledge
Bank reconciliation	Apply the four step method to the information first then answer question	Follow technique
Wages control	Apply the four step method to the information first then answer the question	Follow technique
Errors and the suspense account	Determine the journal that should have been applied. Determine the journal that has been applied Make the adjustment (reverse incorrect journal, input the correct journal)	Follow technique
Reconciliation of control accounts to supplementary ledgers	Reverse the error journal then see if the control account reconciles to the supplementary ledger without the error	Follow technique
Trial Balance Question	Apply money in money out method to determine the direction of money	Application of learnt knowledge/T account technique

The majority of questions in this unit are to be answered using a consistent method that contains three or four parts. However the examiner will:

1) Only ask for information that covers one part of the full technique needed in the hope that students will bypass the whole process that would otherwise guarantee success. For example asking for the items that reconcile the brought forward balances in a bank reconciliation rather than asking for a full bank reconciliation;
2) Include information in the question that is needed to create the answer but not specifically ask a question on it. For example asking for net wages but not gross wages in a Wages Control question; but provide total employers cost as the starting point (gross wages then requiring calculation before getting to net wages).

In both instances the question is determining whether students will attempt to take short-cuts with the necessary technique/make-up their own approach, thereby opening up the possibility of failure. Short-cuts are not required as sufficient time is provided to undertake the full process (and then some). This unit allows students to have 100% knowledge of whether they have passed or failed before they complete the exam (have the answers reconciled – if so you have passed). The phrase "check your work" has a very distinct meaning in this unit, it means perform the technique required to fully know that you have given the right answer by completing all of the reconciliation steps.

Therefore, students who fail this unit take short-cuts, either in:

1) Learning double entry bookkeeping in the Introduction to Bookkeeping unit; or
2) Applying the full techniques for this unit (which in fairness sometimes not appear in other teaching materials for this unit).

In doing so they turn easy high scoring questions (such as the Wages Control question) into low scoring answers. Students complain (after failing) that the examiner's approach has attempted to trick them. To a certain extent it has considered whether they would undermine the control environment of a Finance Department to save their own time. It is important to understand this objective before commencing this unit and be mindful of it whilst learning.

The approach in this book will therefore:

1) Recap double entry bookkeeping, VAT and the five stage accounting system to ensure that learning in this unit is built upon a solid foundation;
2) Teach the required techniques. Workings, as well as the answers, will be provided in this workbook and you should mark your workings more than your answers. If your workings are correct you will always get the answer right in the exam. If you found the answer without the correct workings, today you were right and tomorrow you may drop marks.
3) Provide extensive questioning to reinforce learning. This study guide includes approximately 3 exam assessments worth of exam standard questions.

Chapter 1 Recap of Introduction to Bookkeeping

Before commencing this unit there are three requirements that you should have gained in the Introduction to Bookkeeping unit (which is why that unit must be completed first and this unit immediately after):

1) A strong understanding of the money movements of financial transactions that create debits (positive money) and credits (negative money);
2) How to calculate VAT;
3) To understand the stages of the five stage accountancy system so you can interpret the information given to produce the necessary action (in particular the posting of daybooks to the general ledger and subsidiary ledgers).

For a full recap you should visit the Introduction to Bookkeeping study guide and associated playlist. A short summary is provided here as a refresher.

1.1 Debits and Credits

Accounting systems are based upon fundamental accounting concepts. Two concepts are applicable at level 2:

1) The business entity concept: regardless of structure (and including sole traders) the organisation (company) is separate from its owners;
2) The money measurement concept that only transactions associated with money movements are considered (positive and negative money to the company).

Therefore:

1) If a transaction results in an increase of assets compared to liabilities (a net debit) the shareholders will ultimately receive this at some point in future and there is an equivalent money outflow to those shareholders in the financial transaction (negative money to the company which is an equivalent credit);
2) If a transaction results in a reduction of assets compared to liabilities (a net credit) this reduces the amount available to shareholders at some point in future from any previously accumulated profit or shareholder payments into the company. There is an equivalent money reduction in any future outflow to those shareholders in the financial transaction (positive money to the company which is an equivalent debit).

As a result we have the accounting equation:

Assets = Liabilities + Shareholder Capital

Financial transactions create a flow of money into and out of the company. Positive money into the company is called a debit. Negative money out of the company is called a credit. Debits and credits are only called debits and credits because they were written down in 1494 by Luca Pacioli (who also called debits **money to** the organisation and credits **money by** (money from) the organisation). Debits and credits caught on as the term to be used when it could just have easily been money to and money by (which Luca also stated in his book).

Because we are considering money flows to and from a financial transaction and we have the accounting equation, all money movements in a financial transaction will have two sides (debits and credits) which are represented by the following diagram.

Increasing asset

= increasing money in

= + money

= debit

Increasing liability

= more money out

= - money

= credit

Asset = Liabilities + Capital

Reducing asset

= less money in

= - money

= credit

Reducing liability

= reducing money out

= + money

= debit

You may have passed the Introduction to Bookkeeping unit using the DEAD CLIC mnemonic (or PEARLS). Whilst this was possible due to the questions in that unit you are unlikely to be successful in this unit with that approach as you now need to know why a transaction is a debit or a credit rather than "it just is". If you have used DEAD CLIC it is advisable to read/watch in full the approach to debits and credits in the Introduction to Bookkeeping book/playlist on the YouTube channel. It will save you considerable time.

(1) Double Entry Bookkeeping for AAT Level 2 and AAT Level 3: Paper and cups method - YouTube

1.2 T accounts

In an accountancy system it is important than our numbers add up correctly. A single error makes the whole of our accounting data unreliable (because it could be a very large error in one direction and an almost equivalent error in the other direction such that even small errors have large consequences).

Digital accounting systems have an advantage over manual systems in that they will add correctly however in manual systems we need to introduce checks into the system to:

1) Make it easier to add figures together by splitting longer lists of numbers into smaller lists;
2) Check that our addition is correct.

To do this debits and credits are entered into T accounts with balancing carried down figures as follows:

		Bank			
1/10	b/d	5,000			
6/10	Cash sales	2,000	9/10	HMRC VAT	500
			13/10	Purchases	500
			31/10	c/d	6,000
Total		7,000	Total		7,000
1/11	b/d	6,000			

In a digital accounting system the balance on the account is typically shown as a positive figure for debits and a negative figure for credits (positive and negative money) with a list of transactions creating the final balance (debits less credits as a plus or minus figure). The reason for T accounts that you will see in the exam is because in a manual system:

1) Putting the debits and credits on separate sides means there is less chance of error when adding the numbers up (it is more accurate to add two columns of 20 numbers in each column rather than a single column of 40 numbers) and it is much easier to see what the transaction was (because the other side of the transaction is the description);
2) Including a carried down figure and then retotaling each column to see if the debits now equal the credit is a cross check of whether numbers have been added correctly.

It is important to use T accounts in the exam because they provide the benefits of better addition and clearer workings. This is not "dumbed down" accountancy for lower level qualifications. Professional accountants (in particular partners in practice and older more experienced accountants) will always use T accounts when dissecting a problem in the accounting system or working out what to do.

You will see many control account questions in this unit which are T account questions for assets and liabilities. Any attempt to solve these questions without using T accounts will lose a lot of marks.

1.3 VAT

VAT will appear:

1) In reconciliation questions for ledgers;
2) In error questions;
3) As its own control account question (a T account question).

A lot of marks will be dependent upon an ability to calculate VAT. For any rate of VAT (although it is highly likely in your exam the VAT rate will be 20% or zero in a question).

VAT amount/rate of VAT	=	Net amount
Net amount X rate of VAT	=	VAT amount
Net amount X (rate of VAT + 100%)	=	Gross amount
Gross amount / (rate of VAT +100%)	=	Net Amount
VAT amount	=	Gross amount – net amount

Therefore, where VAT is 20%:

Net amount X 120% = gross amount = Net amount X 1.2

Amount including VAT /120% = Net amount = gross amount /1.2

VAT = Net amount X 20%

VAT is paid to Her Majesty's Revenue & Customs (HMRC) based upon amounts sold to customers (the amounts charged being based upon the net amount) which is collected from the customer and paid by the supplier to HMRC. VAT paid by the company to the supplier on purchases can be reclaimed from HMRC.

VAT must be considered in a T account given there will be movements of amounts owed to HMRC and owed from HMRC based upon sales, purchases, discounts, returns, errors and payments to and from the company.

1.4 The Five Stage Accounting System

The detail of each part of the five stage accounting system forms the majority of the Introduction to Bookkeeping book (so cannot be reproduced in full here). In summary, the flow of information back and forth between the stages is as follows:

What is happening	Type of action	How
Customer discusses prices with supplier	Not a financial transaction	Nothing happens yet
A quotation is provided, prices agreed etc	**Business transaction**	There has been offer of goods or services for a price (consideration).
Customer places order	Purchase order A **business document**	Customer produces purchase order and sends to supplier. Does not go into a day book in a manual system. In a digital system often entered into a commitments section to be later reconciled to invoices received and the delivery/goods in notes and to ensure managers do not exceed budgets.
Supplier sends out goods	Provides a delivery note with goods as proof of what has been dispatched A **business document**	Delivery note is provided with goods. May be other copies held by supplier and courier (although more modern systems have bar coded tracking of deliveries).
Customer checks items and puts in warehouse	Goods inwards note prepared that sets out amounts received and any issues over quality Could include signatures for who accepted the delivery and who checked the quality. A **business document**	The warehouse will prepare the document as verification that it checked the items. It could also have where the items have been stored etc. The delivery note can be checked to the goods inwards note to highlight differences where the supplier has provided different amounts. Both of these documents can be compared to the order to see if the right amounts have been sent as often part orders are sent (and we would not want to pay the full amount in that case)

At this point goods have been delivered		
Supplier prepares the invoice	This is a **business document**. It is the sales invoice for the supplier. For the purchaser it is the purchase invoice. Note they are the same document and are prepared once by the supplier	The supplier wants to be paid so produces a sales invoice setting out the terms, sales taxes (VAT) and other items such as early payment discounts. It might include other amounts to be paid such as delivery charges (carriage) and credit terms (CoD means cash on demand which is pay the delivery driver the money for the items). Two copies are held, one in the supplier (where it is called the sales invoice) and one in the customer (where it is called the purchase invoice)
Supplier enters credit sale in sales day book. Cash sales are entered into the cash book	These are **day books** which collects entries to create a journal. The cashbook may (and most often is) also the general ledger account. Day books are **books of prime entry**.	The sales invoices on credit are entered into the sales day book. They are totaled and entered into: The sales ledger control account VAT control account Sales account In the general ledger And in the customer's account in the sales ledger Cash sales are entered into the cash book (including VAT and sales on the debit side of the cash book).
Customer enters credit sale in the purchases day book and cash purchases in cash book.	These are **day books** which collects entries to create a journal. The cashbook may (and most often is) also the general ledger account. Day books are **books of prime entry**.	The purchase invoices on credit are entered into the purchases day book. They are totaled and entered into: The purchase ledger control account VAT control account Purchase expense account In the general ledger And in the supplier's account in the purchase ledger Cash purchases are entered into the credit

		side of the cash book.
At this point an amount is due for credit sales/purchases and cash sales/purchases have been paid for		
Supplier wants to remind a customer that a debt is owed	Supplier sends customer a supplier statement showing amount due built up of invoices due and previous amounts paid A **statement of account** (if asked it would be a business document)	Information collected from sales ledger and sent to customer. The information is designed to remind the customer what is owed and get them to pay – so it is made easy for the customer to reconcile to their purchase ledger. The customer will use the supplier statement to reconcile what they think is due from their purchase ledger and may question amounts The supplier statement is from the seller's perspective. The purchase ledger is from the buyer's perspective.
Customer pays They enter amount into their cash book	The cashbook is a **day book** and **may also be** used as an account in the **general ledger** (if there is not a separate Bank T account in the general ledger)	Payment made from bank account and entry made into cashbook
Customer reminds supplier they have paid	Customer sends a remittance advice. This is a **business document**	The customer may want to remind a supplier they have paid by sending a remittance advice. This ensures that the supplier stops chasing the debt and may also state amounts deducted for faulty goods or returns or if the company has taken advantage of an early payment discount.
Supplier enters payment for credit sales into their cash book	The cashbook is a **day book** and **may also be** used as a **general ledger** (if there is not a separate Bank T account in the general ledger)	The customer may post this from a remittance advice but is more likely to post it from the bank statement when performing a daily bank reconciliation as the remittance advice would arrive later if at all.
Customer makes cash purchase	Entered into cash day book (which may be a	Supplier and purchaser enters sale/purchase in their respective day books

	cash column in the cash book or a separate day book for cash held/petty cash book)	and then prepare journals into their general ledgers. Note cash sales do not appear in purchase or sales ledgers because there is no debt due. The exception to this may be if the customer wants to track the amounts paid with a particular supplier and may enter it into that supplier's account (with a corresponding immediate payment).
The sales invoice is inaccurate/needs to be changed or there are sales returned (the goods may be faulty). A credit note is issued	The supplier issues a credit note. This is a **business document** and a sales credit note for the seller and purchase credit note for the buyer	The credit note is entered into the sales return day book (a **day book**) for the seller which is then used to create journals to post to the sales ledger control account, sales returns and VAT accounts in the general ledger (a **ledger**) and customer's account in the sales ledger. The purchaser enters the credit note in the purchases returns day book which is used to create journals to post to the purchase ledger control account, purchase returns and VAT accounts in the general ledger and the supplier's account in the purchase ledger.
The purchaser takes advantage of a discount allowed. A credit note may or may not be required (in real life not but the examiner typically assumes it is required).	A credit note may not have to be prepared if there is sufficient information on the invoice. If not a credit note is prepared (**business document**). The customer may note taking advantage of the discount on a remittance advice (**business document**). The examiner typically assumes a credit note is required.	For the seller the discount is entered into the discounts allowed **day book** (book of prime entry) that is used to create journals to post to the sales ledger control account, discounts allowed and VAT accounts in the general ledger (a **ledger**) and customer's account in the sales ledger. For the purchaser the discount is entered into the discounts received **day book** that is used to create journals to post to the purchase ledger control account, discounts received and VAT accounts in the general ledger and the supplier's account in the purchase ledger.
At this point the purchase is paid for and debt cleared		
Bank statement	The bank statement is a	The check is performed via a bank

	statement of account that is used to check the cashbook for missing entries (which are then entered to the cash book) or errors.	reconciliation which has four steps. The cashbook is a day book but most often used as the T account for the bank statement in the general ledger because of the need to perform bank reconciliations.
Petty cash voucher and petty cash book	A staff member may incur expenses to be reclaimed. Their manger will authorise a petty cash voucher which is the **business document**.	The petty cash voucher is posted to the credit side of the petty cash book, which is a **day book** to produce journals that are posted to the petty cash and expenses accounts in the general ledger. If sales are made/cash collected this is entered into the debit side of the petty cashbook
At this point all of the cash accounting journals have been made		
Error is made that needs to be corrected or period end journals required to record stock holdings etc.	Journals are prepared which are entered into a day book called **The Journal** this is a **book of prime entry.**	Posting of journals outside of the more typical day books has increased risk of error and fraud. The more senior accountant will want to control these entries and does so by only allowing them to be posted through a controlled day book (the Journal). The journal required to correct an error may be tested in this unit, the Journal as a book of prime entry is tested in the Principles of Bookkeeping Controls unit.
The general ledger holds all of the company's accounts (T accounts in a manual system). This is used to create the trial balance.	The general ledger holds the balances of the company's different accounts. Other ledgers (such as the sales ledger) provide detail of what makes up the balance of certain control accounts in the general ledger. These are **ledgers**.	The balance brought down is the amount included in the **trial balance** for each ledger. The balanced carried down is used to check the calculation of the brought down figure (by adding up both sides of the T account to determine if they equal one another).
At this point an initial trial balance has been prepared which is used to create financial statements		

Chapter 2 What Is the Objective of Bookkeeping Controls?

Bookkeeping Controls are the foundation upon which the control environment of any organisation is based:

The Wider Control Environment
The organisation's culture with regards to compliance and working for the wider organisation's goals above individual goals

Budget Setting and Variance Analysis
The setting of clear goals and accountability for business units and managers in the organisation

Financial Controls
The checks and processes highlighted in the Introduction to Bookkeeping unit that ensure that financial transactions are correctly authorised and processed

Bookkeeping Controls
Checks accuracy of the processing of financial transactions

Bookkeeping controls are the checks undertaken to ensure the accuracy of the data in our finance system. Without Bookkeeping Controls the financial data will be inaccurate and actions by rogue managers cannot be called into question as the Finance Department has undermined its credibility through inaccurate reporting. As a result, Bookkeeping controls form the foundation for the wider control environment. If they are not effective, the organisation's control environment (and ultimately the way the company conducts business) will be weaker and there will be differences between the values of assets and liabilities in the financial records versus reality.

The majority of the controls in this unit will follow a very specific format. The approach in this book will mirror the workplace where I will set out the process as the professional accountant (being the Finance Director or Financial Controller) and you will implement those controls to the questions and not deviate from the approach.

In each question you will complete the full control first and then take the information from that control to fill in whatever is required to answer the question. Always remember however that the examiner expects you to execute the full control and is only asking for part of the control to trick you into using something else.

Chapter 3 Payment Methods and Treasury Management

Key Points

> There are different methods to pay and receive money.
>
> Each has their advantages and disadvantages and timings that you will need to remember and apply.
>
> For example, a standing order is applicable to a fixed and regular amount; a direct debit is applicable to a variable and regular amount.

This chapter will consider the various methods by which a company may receive or make payments and approaches to treasury management.

3.1 Payment methods

There are many different ways payments can be made and each has its own advantages and disadvantages as well as timings that the payment will take to set up and to process. In the exam you will be:

1) Presented with a scenario and asked to choose the most appropriate payment method;
2) Given a payment method and determine an advantage/disadvantage or the timing of payments;
3) State the payment timing.

The methods of payment are as follows:

Method	Cash, petty cash or Imprest System
	This is physical cash being used to make payments. Small amounts for expenses are typically called petty cash (see petty cash book in Introduction to Bookkeeping).

Advantages	Disadvantages	Timing
Immediate payment received by the company	There is the potential for theft. If large amounts of cash are held the company becomes a target for violent criminals;	Immediate
Very convenient for customers (if they like to use cash)		
	The money has to be banked with associated staff cost.	
Can use petty cash as a system to stop expense claims that have to be processed through wages system (at considerable expense)	There is the need to reconcile cash amount	

Method	**Cheques**
	This is a piece of paper setting out who to be paid (the payee), the amount to be paid, bank account details, date etc. It must be banked by the payee into their account to receive the funds.

Advantages	Disadvantages	Timing
Difficult to steal because it is addressed to a particular payee	Costly to generate (someone has to write it out and reconcile payment at some later date)	? See below
Physical item that can be provided	Costly to bank (it takes time to take to the bank and cash the item)	
Can be posted with a remittance advice		
Can slow up payment for the payer	Time taken to receive in the post (if you are the supplier)	
	The payer may not have the funds in their account so the cheque may bounce	

The timing of cheque payments are now less certain than they once were and the examiner may choose to stay away from this. Traditionally it would be second class post (7 days) and 1 day if the payer and payee banked in the same brank of the same bank as each other or more likely 3 days if the payer and payee used different banks or branches in the same bank. However, with the introduction of cheque scanning by most banks this clearing period is now 1 day but it possible that the exam questions have not caught up with this.

An example of a cheque is here:

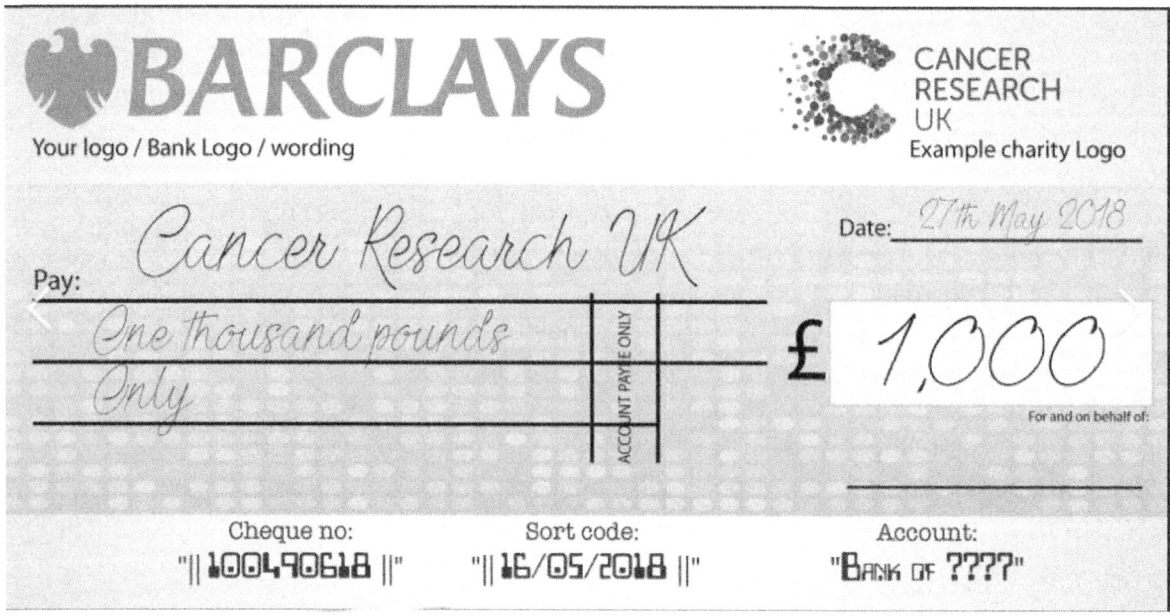

Account payee only means that the cheque can only be cashed into the account named and as a result is harder to steal (if the cheque is sent in the post vs cash).

Method	**Bank draft**		
	Similar to a cheque, this is a piece of paper that can be paid into an account. It has the certainty of payment (the money has been transferred from the account to the draft unlike a cheque which may bounce) so better than a cheque for selling large items like a car.		
Advantages	Disadvantages		Timing
A physical item that can be handed over Certainty that funds exist Potential for it to be fraudulent	Potential for fees Can be cancelled but with a lot of difficulty Potential to be stolen		Immediate (and not likely to be posted given value and potential for theft)

An example of a bank draft is:

Method	**Debit card**	
	This is a card with bank details on it and a form of verification (pin number) to allow the transfer of funds from one bank to another. Debit cards have a short delay for payment with funds being debited from an account (which may be rejected if there is not enough money in the account).	
Advantages	Disadvantages	Timing
Customer convenience Only 1 day delay in receipt of funds	Fixed asset cost to implement Possible card fraud	1 day delay to receiving funds

Method	**Credit cards**		
	This is a card with bank details on it that acts as a credit for payments. There is a credit limit but this amount is not required for payment until a later date.		
Advantages	Disadvantages		Timing
Credit for the customer of up to 1 month

Only 1 day delay for receipt of funds

Customer convenience

Fraud/insolvency protection for customer

Allows employee to pay for items without using their account/the cost of processing expense claims | High transaction charges of typically 1.5-2.5% per transaction (which has reduced over time and is now variable dependent upon the supplier)

High interest rates if debt not settled

May allow expenses that would otherwise be rejected (i.e. alcohol) || For receipt 1 day after transaction
For payment the bill is received at the end of the month for payment (up to 30 days credit) |

Credit card fees are paid by the supplier although they may add this fee onto the cost of the supply. This depends upon the tradition of that industry. Paying for a hotel room is unlikely to result in the fee being passed on whereas paying for £20,000 of computers is likely to result in the fee being charged to the invoice.

Method	**Charge cards/Supplier cards (not referred to in syllabus)**	
	This is a business payments card without the credit element.		
Advantages	Disadvantages	Timing
Allows for purchases to be made without the time expense of going through the finance department – can be cheaper than processing expense claims or operating an imprest system.

May receive procurement rebates with some cards/discounts (effectively a trade discount through using the card).

Only 1 day delay to receipt of funds | Payments require reconciling

May be able to restrict payments to certain items | 1 day after transaction |

Method	**BACS**		
	This is a transfer from one bank account to another. Typically set up as a number of payments to be made at a time (a BACS run) for say paying suppliers or wages.		
Advantages		Disadvantages	Timing
Immediate payment on day BACS payment is set up for Can be cancelled (up to the point of payment) if it is incorrect No transaction costs (although there will be the wider costs as banks will attempt to charge for business accounts that allow BACS payments)		Requires 3 days notice to set up.	Immediate on day

Method	**Faster payments**		
	This is effectively an immediate BACS payments (they use the same system)		
Advantages		Disadvantages	Timing
Immediate payment on the day Does not require advanced notice No bank changes		Payment amount limited (typically up to £100,000 but could £25,000)	2 hours notice

Method	**CHAPS**		
	This uses the faster payments system but is for larger amounts with immediate payment (no 2 hour delay) and cannot be cancelled. Particularly applicable for land/building purposes. House purchases are via CHAPS because of the amounts and because they cannot be cancelled.		
Advantages		Disadvantages	Timing
Immediate payment on day Does not require notice No 2 hour delay as with BACS/Faster Payments Cannot be cancelled No limit for payment amount		Cannot be cancelled Bank charges for processing	Immediate

Method	**Standing Orders** This method of payments uses the BACS or Faster Payments system and sets up a **fixed** payment amount for a preset period or **regular** payment until cancelled. You should look for terms such as "regular fixed amounts" in questions.		
Advantages	Disadvantages		Timing
Gives supplier more confidence they will be paid Effective way of being accurate and making payments on time if the circumstances suit the payment	Can be cancelled by the payer even though as the supplier we feel we have an agreement for payment on a particular date		Immediate on dates of payment

Method	**Direct Debit** This method of payments uses the BACS or Faster Payments system and sets up a **variable** payment amount for a preset period or **regular** payment until cancelled. You should look for terms such as "regular variable amounts" in questions. Given that is allows the supplier to take what they want from the bank account it would only be used for areas such as utility bills, insurance etc. We would never allow a supplier of goods (whose supply could end up in dispute) to have a direct debit.		
Advantages	Disadvantages		Timing
Gives supplier more confidence they will be paid	Can be cancelled by the payer even though as the supplier we feel we have an agreement for payment on a particular date The supplier can now deduct any payment they want to which could be in error or pay for faulty goods/items in dispute.		Immediate on dates of payment

Method	**Mobile phone banking/bank transfers (not referred to in syllabus)** Transfers between banks using a mobile phone app	
Advantages	Disadvantages	Timing
Convenient Immediate	Potential to make mistakes Money out of the account immediately	Immediate

Method	**Direct Credit**		
	Used for regular payments made through BACS system for items such as employee expenses or utilities		
Advantages	Disadvantages		Timing
Payment on day for supplier Can set up regular payments in one go saving time	Potential to make mistakes for example the payment continuing but the employee has left Money out of the account immediately for payer		Immediate

3.2 Treasury Management

It is important that a company understands the timings of its payments in order to always have enough cash in the bank to meet its liabilities as they fall due. A company will always want to:

1) Pay its debts as late as possible; but
2) Not too late so as to:
   a. Miss out on prompt payment discounts;
   b. End up in a situation where a supplier prices late payment into the prices offered or refuses to trade with our company altogether; or
   c. The customer may get bad publicity (for example a supermarket paying its farmers late). The timing of payments to suppliers is reported on in company financial statements.

Some liabilities (such as Her Majesty's Customs and Excise or suppliers who have built penalties into contracts) can charge penalties for late payment. Some suppliers may refuse to take certain types of payment such as credit cards.

Confirmation of Learning

When making a payment we think it will take 7 days for our cheque to arrive at our supplier and be taken to the bank. What is the earliest the funds will leave out bank account in days from posting the cheque?

We intend to pay a fixed amount each month on the same day to a supplier. Which is the most appropriate method of payment – Standing order/Direct debit

We want physical confirmation of the availability of funds in a customer's account before selling them a car. Which is the most appropriate payment we will accept – Cheque/Bank draft

Questions

Question 1 Match the payment method to the situation

Situation	Answer	Potential Payment Methods	
John's Autos wants to be paid in something that is similar to cash but not cash for a car		Faster payments	Cash
Tea and coffee required to be purchased from the local shop		Credit card	Direct Debit
£100 to be paid on the 1st of each month for rental of a garage lock up		Cheque	CHAPS
Variable expenses incurred by a salesperson over the month		Bank draft	Standing order

Question 2 Which two of the following will not reduce funds in the account on the date of payment/posting.

Cheque	Debit card purchase	Bank draft	CHAPS	Credit card purchase

Question 3 Which of the following is a reasonable approach to making payments

Approach	Yes/No
To pay late and wait to be chased before payment	
To pay as late as possible but not late	
To pay a supplier late because they cannot complain about it	
To pay immediately to clear the creditor from the accounts	

Bridge to the next chapter

Because certain payment methods take time to clear the bank account there will typically be a different balance in the bank statement compared to the cashbook. However, it is very important that the cashbook balance is accurate and we use the bank statement to confirm its accuracy.

In the next chapter we will reconcile the cashbook to the bank statement after allowing for the timing of different payments.

Chapter 4 The Bank Statement and Bank Reconciliations

Key Points

Bank reconciliations are the most important bookkeeping control undertaken in any finance department (no finance system can operate without them).

They reconcile the balances in the cashbook to the balances on the bank statement from the bank.

Bank reconciliation questions form 25% of the marks in the exam.

You must follow the same approach at all times. (no matter how the questions are set out in the exam). The approach for every bank reconciliation is always the same despite any different wording or layout in the exam.

A bank reconciliation in the workplace is in four steps

Step 1: reconcile the bfwd balance (in the workplace using the figures from the previous bank reconciliation) ticking off those items in the bank statement

Step 2: tick all of the cashbook items to the bank statement

Step 3: update the cashbook for all of the items in the bank statement that are not in the cashbook

Step 4: reconcile the closing bank statement balance to the revised cashbook

In the exam since you do not have the previous bank reconciliation (which would make the question too easy) you reverse steps 1 and 2 to narrow down the bfwd reconciling items that you must deduce.

Reconcile one transaction to the cashbook to determine the approach being used in the bank statement for the balance on the account.

4.1 The Importance of Cash

Cash (being the balance in the bank account not physical notes and coins) is the most important figure in any set of financial statements. It:

1) Cannot be manipulated, unlike other items, and often highlights where there is an error in the accounting system;
2) Without some cash the company cannot operate;
3) Cash can be used to expand and undertake more profitable opportunities. The amount of available cash is the factor restricting investment;
4) If the company has a period where it does not perform well cash provides a buffer of time to restructure the business.

Senior managers and overseers will tend to use cash holdings as guide for general performance and company risk. It is vital that the cash figure in the accounting system is accurate and this figure will be subject to the most frequent checks for accuracy.

However:

1) There will be items in the bank account, such as bank charges or refused cheques, that we would not know about unless we reviewed the bank statement. They may not be in the cashbook;
2) In chapter 3 we considered the timing of receipts and payments and noted that whilst we may have undertaken some financial transactions (which we would then record in the cashbook) they may not clear the bank account until some later time;
3) There could be errors in the transactions or entries into the cash daybook.

We need a mechanism to find these differences and adjust the cashbook if necessary to create the accurate cash holding. We also want to confirm that the bank account balance in the general ledger is free from error. To do this we perform a bank reconciliation which reconciles the bank account balance in the general ledger (also referred to as the cash balance) to the bank statement from the bank.

4.2 Exam Technique

You will typically perform 3 bank reconciliations in the exam for 25% of the marks. You will not pass without being able to perform a bank reconciliation. However, there is a simple and straightforward approach to answering every bank reconciliation question regardless of the different approaches the examiner adopts.

Given this simple approach how do students fail a bank reconciliation question?

Failure occurs because the examiner will only ask for figures from part of the bank reconciliation even though the marks will give sufficient time for the full reconciliation to be produced. Students who fail this question then try to:

1) Take short-cuts to producing the answer;
2) Make up a different approach which leads to errors; or
3) Because they have not completed the full reconciliation have not spotted an arithmetical error in their workings. Preparing the bank reconciliation checks the answer to the question (if your bank reconciliation reconciles the available figures must be correct which you then slot into the answer).

Essentially those students have been tricked into not preparing a full bank reconciliation although the subsequent failure is of their own making

Instead you must always produce the full reconciliation for the question and only then attempt to answer the question. If your bank reconciliation reconciles you will know that any balance you take from it will be correct. If it does not reconcile you will know that somewhere you have made an arithmetical error. You will not have this check if you attempt to short-cut this question and not perform the full reconciliation (which you are given the time for in the exam).

To provide an example a question may ask:

Task 6 (10 marks)

The bank statement and cash book for May are shown below.

Check the bank statement against the cash book and enter:

- **any transactions into the cash book as needed**
- **the cash book balance carried down at 31 May and brought down at 1 June.**

Which is only asking for an adjustment to the cashbook (not produce the bank reconciliation) when a full bank reconciliation is required to answer the question and check if the answer is correct.

4.3 The Four Steps of a Bank Reconciliation

The process of reconciling a bank statement to the cash book in the workplace is as follows:

Step 1	**Reconcile the brought forward balance** in the cash book to the brought forward amount in the bank statement. This will be by taking the previous bank reconciliation and ticking off the outstanding lodgments (money we think we have paid in but not yet cleared the bank statement) and unpresented cheques (money we think we have paid out but not yet cleared the bank statement) in that bank reconciliation	The differences between the brought forward balances will have **already** been posted in the cash book last month. They will be cheques and deposits that were in the cash book in the previous point of reconciliation but had not cleared in the bank by that point. If they were posted again to the cashbook via step 3 as adjustments this would double post them in error.
Step 2	**Tick all of the payments and receipts in the cashbook to the bank statement** noting any in the cashbook that cannot be found – these are outstanding lodgements, unpresented cheques or errors where different amounts were actually received/paid than stated in the cashbook.	These items are in the cashbook and have cleared in the bank statement. We do not need to do anything with them. In the exam it is unlikely that there will be errors in posting to the cashbook (i.e. the same transaction but posted incorrectly to the cashbook and therefore a different figure in the bank statement).
Step 3	**Update the cashbook** for any items in the bank statement that are not ticked in the cashbook. This will include any bounced cheques.	We will need to adjust the cashbook for any receipts or payments we did not know about. For example, interest received, a customer payment or a bounced cheque. We may also find errors that require adjustment.

			The adjusted cashbook is the new bank balance for the trial balance.
Step 4	**Reconcile the bank statement to the adjusted cash book** noting		Start with the balance in the bank statement figure.
	1) Outstanding lodgements – which are monies in, receipts, the cashbook that has not yet appeared in the bank statement		Add on any outstanding lodgements – these need to be added to increase the bank statement amount to the amounts in the cash book
	2) Uncleared cheques – which are monies out, payments, in the cashbook that has not yet cleared in the bank statement And check that this reconciled figure is the same as the cashbook		Take off any unpresented cheques – these need to be taken off the bank statement balance because they are in the cashbook but not in the bank statement and they are payments

Due to the need to tick the cashbook to the bank statement steps 2 and 3 in the bank reconciliation effectively require the cashbook to be the ledger account in a manual system as well as the daybook (it would be too messy otherwise to perform a bank reconciliation).

In an exam you are unlikely to be given the previous bank reconciliation. The reason is that this would provide you with the template to answer the question (everyone then getting it right). You will still need to do the steps in a bank reconciliation but in a different order being:

Step 1 – tick the cashbook to the bank statement;

Step 2 - reconcile the opening balances

Step 3 - adjust the cashbook

Step 4 - reconcile the bank statement to the adjusted cash book

In an exam steps 1 and 2 are reversed because there are now less items to add together to try and reconcile the opening balances. The bfwd reconciling items will typically be unticked items around the start of the month in the bank statement. To see some examples of bank reconciliations watch:

Bank reconciliations four examples AAT level 2 Bookkeeping Controls - YouTube

4.4 The Bank Statement

For bank reconciliation questions you will be provided with a bank statement and cashbook for the organisation. Students are often confused initially because the bank statement is set out as the opposite of the cashbook where Positive money is a credit and Negative money is a debit.

Bank Statement from Bank of Norton				Company Bank Account in General Ledger			
			Balance	Debits	£	Credits	£
Starting balance	credit		1,020	Balance b/d	1,020		
Payment out 1	debit	46	974			Payment out 1	46
Payment in 1	credit	51	1,025	Payment in 1	51		
Payment out 2	debit	70	955			Payment out 2	70
Payment in 2	credit	94	1,049	Payment in 2	94		
Payment in 3	credit	56	1,105	Payment in 3	56		
Payment out 3	debit	67	1,038			Payment out 3	67
Payment in 4	credit	73	1,111	Payment in 4	73		
Payment out 4	debit	47	1,064			Payment out 4	47
Payment out 5	debit	65	999			Payment out 5	65
Payment in 5	credit	70	1,069	Payment in 5	70		
Payment out 6	debit	33	1,036			Payment out 6	33
Closing balance	credit		1,036			Balance c/d	1,036
				Total	1,364	Total	1,364
				Balance b/d	1,036		

On the bank statement payments in to increase the balance held are often stated as credits and payments out to reduce the balance held are debits. This is the opposite as stated in the bank account in the company's accounting system where increases in the asset are debits and reduction in this asset are credits. The reason for this is because the bank statement is from the bank's, not your, perspective. As a result, if it is in credit it means the bank owes you money and is negative money out to you (from the bank's perspective) in the future. Because you are owed money by the bank in your accounting system this is positive money and a debit.

Whilst this does not seem very customer friendly to change this approach now would cause chaos as the whole world is used to this approach. However, the bank statement might be stated as positive money (which would be a debit in the cashbook) or negative money (a credit in the cashbook). You may see different types of bank statements, some with debits and credits and others with positive and negative balances. The debits and credits statements are as stated above. The positive and negative balance statements are the same as the cashbook (with positive balances being debits and negative balances being credits).

It is also possible that the balance from the bank statement is removed requiring you to add up the bank statement in order to have the balance for your bank reconciliation. There will be a number of different ways the questions will be set out (typically two or three) and if you want to get used to the different options practice the exam assessments with the accompanying practice assessments to this book. The method in the exam to adopt is to reconcile one transaction from the bank statement to the cashbook to determine how the bank statement is treating the balances.

4.5 Example of Bank Reconciliation

The company has the following bank statement and cashbook:

Bank Statement			
The Bank of Norton West			
Date	Detail	Transaction	Balance
01/03/2022	Bfwd	301 DR	301 DR
04/03/2022	Invoice X709203	74 CR	227 DR
07/03/2022	Invoice X709210	90 CR	137 DR
09/03/2022	Invoice X709205	6 CR	131 DR
11/03/2022	Hence Metal Windows	91 DR	222 DR
12/03/2022	Sun Mortgage Co	41 DR	263 DR
15/03/2022	Invoice X709206	70 CR	193 DR
15/03/2022	Invoice X709204	84 CR	109 DR
16/03/2022	Good View Collective	85 DR	194 DR
16/03/2022	Catenary Coal Co	67 DR	261 DR
19/03/2022	Invoice X709207	96 CR	165 DR
21/03/2022	Camelot Amazon	6 DR	171 DR
23/03/2022	Glass Windows	12 DR	183 DR
24/03/2022	Invoice X709209	3 CR	180 DR
25/03/2022	Clear Appeal	78 DR	258 DR
27/03/2022	Invoice X709208	69 CR	189 DR

Cashbook					
Date	Detail	Amount	Date	Detail	Amount
			01/03/22	bfwd	379
09/03/22	Invoice X709205	6	11/03/22	Hence Metal Windows	91
15/03/22	Invoice X709206	70	01/03/22	Glass Advantage	87
19/03/22	Invoice X709207	96	21/03/22	Camelot Amazon	6
24/03/22	Invoice X709209	3	23/03/22	Glass Windows	12
27/03/22	Invoice X709208	69	12/03/22	Sun Mortgage Co	41
15/03/22	Invoice X709204	84			
31/03/22	cfwd	288			
	Total	616		Total	616

In the exam the bank statement will use different layouts such as debits and credits or account balances (plus and minus balances). You should first work out how the bank statement is set out by comparing one of the payments into the bank statement to the cashbook to determine what is being used.

The steps to **every** bank reconciliation question are as follows:

Step 1 in the exam tick all of the cashbook items to the bank statement

Bank Statement The Bank of Norton West			
Date	Detail	Transaction	Balance
01/03/2022	Bfwd	301 DR	301 DR
04/03/2022	Invoice X709203	74 CR	227 DR
07/03/2022	Invoice X709210	90 CR	137 DR
09/03/2022	Invoice X709205	6 CR	131 DR
11/03/2022	Hence Metal Windows	91 DR	222 DR
12/03/2022	Sun Mortgage Co	41 DR	263 DR
15/03/2022	Invoice X709206	70 CR	193 DR
15/03/2022	Invoice X709204	84 CR	109 DR
16/03/2022	Good View Collective	85 DR	194 DR
16/03/2022	Catenary Coal Co	67 DR	261 DR
19/03/2022	Invoice X709207	96 CR	165 DR
21/03/2022	Camelot Amazon	6 DR	171 DR
23/03/2022	Glass Windows	12 DR	183 DR
24/03/2022	Invoice X709209	3 CR	180 DR
25/03/2022	Clear Appeal	78 DR	258 DR
27/03/2022	Invoice X709208	69 CR	189 DR

Cashbook					
Date	Detail	Amount	Date	Detail	Amount
			01/03/22	bfwd	379
09/03/22	Invoice X709205	6	11/03/22	Hence Metal Windows	91
15/03/22	Invoice X709206	70	01/03/22	Glass Advantage	87
19/03/22	Invoice X709207	96	21/03/22	Camelot Amazon	6
24/03/22	Invoice X709209	3	23/03/22	Glass Windows	12
27/03/22	Invoice X709208	69	12/03/22	Sun Mortgage Co	41
15/03/22	Invoice X709204	84			
31/03/22	cfwd	288			
	Total	616		Total	616

This reduces the number of options that could be the difference between the brought forward balances on the cashbook and bank statement. The unticked items in the cashbook will be used in step 4 to create the bank reconciliation.

Step 2 reconcile the bfwd balances to see what was in the cashbook in the previous period but not in the bank statement (but now in the bank statement). Tick off these items in the bank statement.

Previous months bank reconciliation
Balance per bank statement		-301
Add outstanding lodgements		
Invoice X709203	74	
Total		74
Less unpresented cheques		
Good View Collective	-85	
Catenary Coal Co	-67	
		-152
Balance on cashbook		-379

Our ticked bank statement now looks like

Bank Statement The Bank of Norton West			
Date	Detail	Transaction	Balance
01/03/2022	Bfwd	301 DR	301 DR
04/03/2022	Invoice X709203	74 CR	227 DR
07/03/2022	Invoice X709210	90 CR	137 DR
09/03/2022	Invoice X709205	6 CR	131 DR
11/03/2022	Hence Metal Windows	91 DR	222 DR
12/03/2022	Sun Mortgage Co	41 DR	263 DR
15/03/2022	Invoice X709206	70 CR	193 DR
15/03/2022	Invoice X709204	84 CR	109 DR
16/03/2022	Good View Collective	85 DR	194 DR
16/03/2022	Catenary Coal Co	67 DR	261 DR
19/03/2022	Invoice X709207	96 CR	165 DR
21/03/2022	Camelot Amazon	6 DR	171 DR
23/03/2022	Glass Windows	12 DR	183 DR
24/03/2022	Invoice X709209	3 CR	180 DR
25/03/2022	Clear Appeal	78 DR	258 DR
27/03/2022	Invoice X709208	69 CR	189 DR

Step 3 update the cashbook for the missing items that are on the bank statement but not in the cashbook:

				bfwd	288
07/03/22	Invoice X709210	90	25/03/22	Clear Appeal	78
31/03/22	cfwd	276			
	Total	982		Total	982
			01/04/22	bfwd	276

All of the bank statement items are now in the cashbook. Such that the difference between the cashbook and the bank statement should now only be things in the cashbook that are not on the bank statement.

Step 4 reconcile the bank statement to the cashbook to compare the bank statement balance plus the unticked cashbook items in step 1 to the cashbook balance. Note in this question the bank balance is given to you but you may need to add up the statement yourself in some questions:

Cashbook

Date	Detail	Amount	Date	Detail	Amount
			01/03/22	bfwd	379
09/03/22	Invoice X709205	6	11/03/22	Hence Metal Windows	91
15/03/22	Invoice X709206	70	01/03/22	Glass Advantage	87
19/03/22	Invoice X709207	96	21/03/22	Camelot Amazon	6
24/03/22	Invoice X709209	3	23/03/22	Glass Windows	12
27/03/22	Invoice X709208	69	12/03/22	Sun Mortgage Co	41
15/03/22	Invoice X709204	84			
31/03/22	cfwd	288			
	Total	616		Total	616

				bfwd	288
07/03/22	Invoice X709210	90	25/03/22	Clear Appeal	78
31/03/22	cfwd	276			
	Total	982		Total	982
			01/04/22	bfwd	276

Bank Reconciliation

Balance per bank statement	-189
Add outstanding lodgements	
Total	0
Less unpresented cheques	
Glass Advantage	-87
	-87
Balance per updated cashbook	-276

In the workplace step 1 and step 2 are reversed (because you already have the previous period's bank reconciliation). It is also possible (in fact likely) that items in the previous bank reconciliation have still not cleared the bank statement (as companies often perform daily or weekly bank reconciliations). The items in that bank statement that have not yet cleared the bank statement are added to the next bank reconciliation (you will not see this in the exam because you will not be given the previous bank reconciliation although it would make for a different and more realistic question).

Note how in a bank reconciliation the bank statements and cashbook balances are stated as positive and negative money. Positive for debits in the cashbook and negative for credits. This follows the money in money out method for double entry bookkeeping and is the correct approach. It is also the method adopted for account balances in digital systems.

> **Confirmation of learning**
>
> What are the 4 steps to a bank reconciliation?
>
> Is it possible to skip a step in the exam if the answer allows it?

Question 1 ABC Ltd performs its bank reconciliation monthly. Below is the bank statement and cashbook for the month of March. What was the bank reconciliation for the month of February?

Bank Statement The Bank of Norton West				
Date		Detail	Debit	Credit
	01/03/2022	Bfwd	973	
	02/03/2022	Invoice X523511		41
	02/03/2022	Invoice X523504		78
	04/03/2022	Invoice X523508		83
	06/03/2022	Smarty Life	56	
	07/03/2022	Sparkle loan & Savings	55	
	08/03/2022	Invoice X523507		39
	08/03/2022	Invoice X523505		63
	09/03/2022	FrontMax Windows	94	
	14/03/2022	Invoice X523506		44
	14/03/2022	Expansion Place	94	
	16/03/2022	Catenary Coal Co	14	
	19/03/2022	Invoice X523510		86
	21/03/2022	LovelyAmazon	98	
	21/03/2022	Invoice X523509		42

Cashbook					
Date	Detail	Amount	Date	Detail	Amount
			01/03/22	bfwd	989
14/03/22	Invoice X523506	44	07/03/22	Sparkle loan & Savings	55
08/03/22	Invoice X523507	39	03/03/22	Moments Count	53
04/03/22	Invoice X523508	83	14/03/22	Expansion Place	94
19/03/22	Invoice X523510	86	16/03/22	Catenary Coal Co	14
21/03/22	Invoice X523509	42	06/03/22	Smarty Life	56
08/03/22	Invoice X523505	63			
31/03/22	cfwd	904			
	Total	1261		Total	1261

Bridge to the next chapter

Bank reconciliations highlight items which are missing from the cashbook. In the next chapter we will consider the other potential errors that can occur in an accounting system and their impact upon the trial balance.

Chapter 5 Why Errors Occur – Classification of Errors and Impact Upon the Trial Balance

> **Key Points**
>
> Errors can occur in both manual and digital accounting systems. In the exam you will typically be asked to:
>
> Determine whether an error in the system will result in the trial balance no longer tallying (the debits no longer being equal to the credits);
>
> Classify the name of the error (each type of error has different name);
>
> Calculate the journal required to fix an error and clear a suspense account;
>
> Select which scenario may have created the error stated.
>
> To be able to answer the questions you must have a good grasp of double entry bookkeeping.

Bookkeeping controls are design to confirm the accuracy of our accounting system and highlight where an error occurs.

Errors are most easily learnt through highlighting the type of questions you may be asked and then considering how those errors may be found or addressed. In this chapter we will consider how errors occur and are classified. In the next chapter we will fix errors using suspense accounts and journals posted through a daybook called The Journal.

Before starting chapters 4 and 5 you should have a strong grasp of:

1) Debits and credits (positive money and negative money to the company);
2) The five stage accounting system's documents, daybooks, ledgers and trial balance.

You should refresh your Introduction to Bookkeeping knowledge regularly until this becomes second nature to you.

5.1 Types of Error

In the exam you will typically be presented with an error(s) and:

1) Determine if it will result in the trial balance tallying (the debits still equal the credits even though the individual accounts are incorrect) or not;
2) Classifying those errors – giving them a name. Typically you will only name errors that do not effect the trial balance.

5.1.1 If the balance sheet balances why does it matter?

If there is an error in our accounting system, even if it did not create an imbalance between the debits and credits in our trial balance it can still have large (called material) implications for the operations of our business. The error could:

1) Change to totals of our accounting equation:

Assets = Liabilities + Capital

For example putting a motor vehicle expense (a capital account) into motor vehicles assets (an asset account). In this instance the assets are now overstated (there is no new vehicle it was petrol that has been used);

2) Omit (leave out) the journal in its entirety or be a wrong but still balancing amount. Again our trial balance tallies but is not reflective of the true values that have occurred and gives a misleading picture to any reviewer;

3) The amounts may be in the correct type of account (for example posted into the sales ledger) but to the wrong account holder such that we think one customer has paid when they have not and another customer has not paid when they have.

In the workplace it is vital that staff members are conscientious in their operations, understand that errors can occur, follow/adjust systems to minimise errors and check for errors. In the exam you will be required to name the error, in the workplace the important thing is to eliminate and address every error.

The types of error in an accounting system are as follows:

5.2 Errors where the trial balance will still tally

5.2.1 Error of Omission

An error of omission is a financial transaction that is missing from the accounting system. For example a credit note not included in a day book and therefore not posted to the ledgers.

Errors of omission are typically found when comparing ledger accounts to statements of account such as remittance advice from customers, supplier statements from suppliers or when reconciling the bank account. Because there is no entry in the ledgers for these errors the company's trial balance will still balance/tally (the debits and credits being equal to each other). This is because both the debit and credit of this transaction are missing.

5.2.2 Error of Principle

An error of principle is where a key principle in accounting is broken through the error and the result is no longer in accordance with generally agreed accounting principle (GAAP) (either because it breaks accounting rules or the company's own policy for applying those rules). The debit and credit entries are the same but the account to which that debit or credit is posted to is:

1) Fundamentally different in type than the account it should have been posted to; or
2) A company's accounting policy (an approach used to create the financial statements) is broken. The items where this could occur (depreciation and stock) appear at level 3 such that this will not be tested in this unit.

An example of an error of principle would be posting a vehicle purchase to a vehicle expense account rather than to vehicles at cost account.

The easiest way to consider if a transaction is an error of principle for this unit is:

Convert the two general ledger accounts involved in the error, where it is and where is should be, into:

1) Assets;
2) Liabilities;
3) Capital.

If the two accounts are different (for example a vehicle purchase –being an asset- and vehicle expenses being a capital account) this is an error of principle as it is against the accounting principle.

The journal created under an error of principle balances and therefore errors of principle do not result in a trial balance not tallying (balancing). They are found from a review of the trial balance (typically seeing whether assets or liabilities are over/understated when comparing to statements of account or to physical verification of the asset/liability). In real life this is through the professional accountant reconciling back to physical verification checks (such as comparing the fixed asset register to actual items).

Note this is an error of princi**ple** not princi**pal** (which is either the original amount of a loan agreed to be paid back or the head of a college).

5.2.3 Error of Commission

This is where the amounts are posted to the wrong account but it does not lead to an error of principle. For example posting an amount to the wrong customer in the sales ledger or posting an amount to the wrong asset (for example fixtures and fittings rather than computer equipment). Again there is no imbalance in the journal posted such that the trial balance will still balance. To determine this follow the same approach as the error of principle but errors of commission remain within the same overall categories of assets, liabilities and capital.

5.2.4 Error of Original Entry

This error is where the figure is entered into accounts incorrectly. The debits and credits are still equal (so this is not picked up by the trial balance being unequal) but the amount is incorrect over or understanding the financial transaction. For example:

Actual amounts entered	Amounts that should have been entered
Dr Sales Ledger Control Account £120	Dr Sales Ledger Control Account £210
Cr VAT £20	Cr VAT £35
Cr Sales £100	Cr Sales £175

5.2.5 Error of reversal

For this error the financial transaction is posted to the correct accounts but the debits are posted as credits and vice versa. The amounts move the accounts in the wrong direction (and have to be reversed before the correct posting is made). Since the original journal balances the error will not result in a difference in the trial balance.

In the exam you will typically see errors of reversal when reconciling purchase and sales ledgers to their control accounts in the general ledger (the daybook being posted the wrong way around).

Actual amounts entered	Amounts that should have been entered
Cr Sales Ledger Control Account £120	Dr Sales Ledger Control Account £120
Dr VAT £20	Cr VAT £20
Dr Sales £100	Cr Sales £100

5.2.6 Compensating Error

A compensating error is where there are two or more journals whose errors cancel each other out. As a result, the trial balance will still balance yet there are multiple errors in our accounts. In the workplace compensating errors that match are rare but offsetting errors (where an error in one direction offsets the error in the other direction) are not. Any difference in the trial balance debits and credits therefore has the potential to be multiples of much larger errors requiring their investigation, however small.

5.3 Errors that result in the trial balance not tallying

The following errors will result in the debits not equaling the credits in a trial balance:

5.3.1 Transposition Error and Different Credits and Debits

A transposition error and different credits and debits is where the journal has been transposed incorrectly to one or both sides of the journal, which no longer balances. Because the journal doesn't balance the trial balance will no longer balance and/or the control account will not balance to the supplementary ledger (for example posting a different amount from the day book into the sales ledger compared to the sales ledger control account). This can arise from miscasting (miscounting) the total of a day book such that the amounts posted are different.

5.3.2 Single Sided Errors or Two Errors on the Same Side of the Journal

In this error only one side of the journal is posted or both sides are posted to the same side (two sets of debits rather than a debit and a credit for example) leading to an imbalance in the trial balance.

5.3.3 Miscasting error

This is an error from arithmetic that results in the trial balance not balancing. For example, adding up a T account incorrectly to produce the wrong bfwd balance.

5.3.4 Extracting of Trial Balance Error

In this error the wrong amounts have been extracted from the accounts to produce the trial balance and the trial balance will not tally.

5.4 Summary of Errors that affect and do not affect the trial balance

One method of searching for errors is to see if the trial balance tallies (both sides equal one another). However, this only finds errors where journal(s) posted to the general ledger do not have equal debit and credit amounts and those journals do not compensate for one another. The errors that affect and do not affect the trial balance are as follows:

Errors that affect the trial balance	Errors that do not affect the trial balance
Errors of Transposition	Errors of Principle
Single Sided Entry	Errors of Commission
Different Values of Debits and Credits in a Journal	Compensating Errors
Two Entries on the Same Side	Reversal of Entries
Miscasting Errors	Errors of Omission
Extracting Errors	Errors of Original Entry

Confirmation of Learning

If the debits and the credits in the trial balance equal one another our accounting system is free from errors. True/False?

For the debits and credits in the trial balance to not equal each other the journal(s) that led to the error must have debits that do not equal credits. True/False?

If an accounting system finds an error whose debits do not equal credits the trial balance must not be in balance. True/False?

Bridge to the next chapter

In the next chapter you will be presented with errors which create an imbalance in the trial balance and correct those errors using a suspense account and journals through a daybook called The Journal.

Questions

Question 1

Assign the correct classification to the following errors:

Error	Classification
Two or more errors occur whose debits do not equal credits but their effect on the trial balance cancel each other out	
A loan repayment is credited to payment of shareholder capital	
£600 payment by A Jones Plumbers is credited to A Johns Ltd in the sales ledger	
The Sales Daybook is posted to the general ledger as Debit Sales £1000 Debit VAT £200 Credit Sales Ledger Control Account £1200	

Options		
Error of Principle	Reversal of Entries	Compensating Errors
Error of Commission	Error of Omission	Error of Original Entry

Question 2

Which of the following errors cause the trial balance to no longer balance?

Error	Will cause and imbalance in the trial balance (Yes/No)
A cash purchase is posted to the purchases and VAT accounts only	
A purchase of a motor vehicle has been posted to the motor expense account instead. All other entries are correct.	
A customer receipt was debited to the sales ledger control account and credited to the bank account	
A petty cash expense for £15 was posted as £51 to the analysis column in the petty cash book but as £15 in the total column.	

Chapter 6 Suspense Accounts and The Journal

> **Key Points**
>
> Where there is an error that results in the trial balance no longer tallying a suspense account is created for the difference. The imbalance results from an incorrect journal whose debits do not equal credits.
>
> This account is then returned to zero (cleared) by reversing the incorrect journal(s) with the suspense account entry making up the difference between the debits and credits in the incorrect journal.
>
> The correct journal is then entered.
>
> Correcting journals posted in error are processed through a daybook called The Journal. This includes all of the other low volume journals such as writing off an irrecoverable debt (at level 3 you will see it is used for extended trial balance entries such as year-end stock or depreciation).

Where the trial balance does not balance this needs to be corrected. However, the original errors are not rubbed out and re-entered in a manual or digital accounting system as this:

1) Would be messy and may not be possible (for example ink cannot move down a page in a manual book to fit in the new journal)
2) The professional accountants in the organisation want to see who made the errors and implement any necessary changes to the controls.

Instead a temporary suspense (error) account is set up and journals are posted to fix the error. In fixing the error (reversing the incorrect journal entries and posting the correct entries) the suspense account is cleared. This is one type of journal that might be posted via The Journal and is why these entries and this day book are controlled by a more senior accountant.

The steps to create and then clear a suspense account are as follows:

1) A suspense account is prepared with an entry that is the difference between the two sides of the trial balance. The two sides of the trial balance are retotaled to check they now equal one another;
2) The original journal is reversed. However, because this contained an error the two sides of the journal do not equal each other. The difference between the two sides is made up with an amount that will be posted to the suspense account in the reversal of the incorrect journal;
3) The new correct journal is posted (if required) for the actual transaction whose debits equals credits.

Example:

A Sales Daybook has been posted as:

Cr Sales £100

Cr VAT £20

But the trade receivables control account (Dr £120) was missed. The trial balance is totaled and the totals are:

| Dr £10,000 | Cr £10,120 |

The difference is £120 which must be added to the debit side in a suspense account:

Suspense Account

| Dr | £120 | |

The journal created in error is reversed:

Dr Sales £100

Dr VAT £20

Cr Suspense £120

Suspense Account

| Dr | £120 | Cr £120 |

This clears the suspense account.

The correct journal is then posted

Dr Trade receivables control account £120

Cr Sales £100

Cr VAT £20

In the exam there will typically be two journals posted in error so it is important to maintain a T account for the suspense account in your workings to see that overall the suspense account is cleared when you post both of the journals to reverse the error.

There may be an attempt to short-cut this approach by merely posting the differences between the original and correct journals to the accounts and the opposite side to the suspense account. However, this would be poor practice in real life as:

1) It is not clear what business document the journal entry is coming from. Instead two journals have to be combined making it difficult to reconcile back to the original business document (and in real life this irritates senior managers and auditors

considerably as they can no longer trace an entry back to a sales invoice for example);
2) The correction aggregates a series of calculations and is less likely to be accurate/hold up under the pressure of an exam. As accountants we constantly strive for approaches that disaggregate numbers to improve accuracy.

It is far easier to reverse the whole of the original incorrect journal and reverse the suspense account and then post the correct journal.

The exam can ask for either approach (reversing and then correctly posting or posting the difference) and the way to recognise this is to see how much space you are left for journals (i.e. space for two journals which would be reverse and then post the correct journal or only one journal which would be the net difference).

If you are unsure of a net difference journal.

1) prepare the reversing and new correct journal separately

Dr Sales £100

Dr VAT £20

Cr Suspense £120

And

Dr Trade receivables control account £120

Cr Sales £100

Cr VAT £20

2) cancel out as much as you can

~~Dr Sales £100~~

~~Dr VAT £20~~

Cr Suspense £120

And

Dr Trade receivables control account £120

~~Cr Sales £100~~

~~Cr VAT £20~~

3) the net difference journal is the items left

Dr Trade receivables control account £120

Page 44

Cr Suspense £120

6.1 The Journal

In the Introduction to Bookkeeping unit journals to the general ledger were posted using the day books that have high volumes of transactions such as sales/purchases day books, the cashbook and petty cashbook. Those day books collected volumes of information on sales or purchases etc to post this volume as a single journal rather than lots of individual sales or purchases. For a manual system this reduces the number of journals to be posted to the ledgers (reducing the risk of error) and allows many finance staff to work on the accounting books and ledgers at the same time. In a digital system the day books are not needed and entries are made individually direct to the ledgers.

But what about financial transactions that only happen occasionally for example an irrecoverable debt, a provision for doubtful debts or journals to reverse errors and clear a suspense account? Do we have to invent a day book for every different type of transaction?

All of the low volume transactions are posted in a book of prime entry called The Journal. The title of this daybook often confuses students as the other books of prime entry (daybooks) are used to create journals. This name should be considered as follows:

1) All books of prime entry create journals
2) The Journal is a book of prime entry to create and record special journals. This day book must be carefully controlled due to the risk of error and potential for fraud.

The journals that are included in the Journal are special as they are adjusting our general ledger without being in the normal course of business via making sales or purchases or receiving or making payments etc. Instead they reflect items such as writing off an irrecoverable debt, period end journals or correcting an error.

The journals that are created via The Journal have the potential to:

1) Introduce errors in the system if inexperienced staff are allowed to post them, often creating journals that do not balance or are incorrect;
2) Manipulate the accounts to perpetrate fraud, for example telling a customer to pay into a different bank account (controlled by the fraudster) and writing off the debt via a journal.

In a manual system, a more senior accountant (typically the Financial Controller or Finance Director) would control this type of journal and they would keep hold of this special book of prime entry. In a digital system the system is password protected with only certain users having the authority to post journals of this type. Auditors would review journals in The Journal in detail given their high risk.

> **Confirmation of learning**
>
> A suspense account is created where the total of debits does not equal the total of credits in a trial balance. True/False?
>
> How is the suspense account cleared?
>
> Which daybook are the journals posted to clear a suspense account entered into?

Questions

Question 1

ABC Ltd has posted two journals in error (there is no VAT)

	Dr	Cr
Journal 1	Trade receivables £1,000	Sales £100
Journal 2	Purchases £200	Trade Payables £2,000

What amount will be in the suspense account before these journals are corrected?

	Dr	Cr
Suspense		

The total of debits in the trial balance is £100,000 before the suspense account is created. What is the total of debits and credits after the suspense account is created?

	Dr	Cr
Total of trial balance		

Question 2

The totals extracted from the trial balance are as follows:

	Dr	Cr
Total of trial balance	£98,000	100,000

A suspense account should be created for:

	Dr	Cr
Suspense		

Correcting which of the following errors would clear the suspense account:

Error	Would help clear	Would not help clear
An error omitting a sales invoice from the sales daybook		
A single sided entry in a journal		
An error of commission		
An error where VAT on a purchase had been incorrectly entered into the daybook as £120 rather than £210. All other entries being correct.		

Bridge to the next chapter

In chapters 4 and 5 we learnt that errors can occur and how to fixed them when they happen. In chapter 3 we reconciled the cashbook to the bank statement as one method of finding errors. In the next chapter we will reconcile the trade receivables control account to the sales ledger and the trade payables control account to the purchase ledger to find other errors.

Suspense account questions are reviewed further in section 8.3.

Chapter 7 Trade Receivables and Trade Payables Control Account Reconciliations

> **Key Points**
>
> The Trade Receivables Control Account is reconciled to the Sales Ledger.
>
> The Trade Payables Control Account is reconciled to the Purchase Ledger.
>
> If there is a difference between them it is an error. In the exam you will typically be asked to pick which scenario created the error.
>
> There is a 4 step process to determining the exam question answer which converts the potential for mental arithmetic to go wrong into a certain answer.
>
> Alternative question – what is the balance – requires good knowledge of T accounts and posting from daybooks.

In the Introduction to Bookkeeping unit you will have become familiar with:

1) Control accounts for Trade Receivables and Trade Payables;
2) A sales ledger which breaks down the Trade Receivables into each customer's account;
3) A purchase ledger which breaks down the Trade Payables into each supplier's account;
4) Supplier statements stating what the supplier believes the amount due is;
5) Remittance advice from customers stating what they are paying and the balance they believe is on the account;
6) Posting via daybooks to the general ledger control accounts and to the sales and purchase ledger.

If you are not familiar with these terms you must return to the Introduction to Bookkeeping book to obtain this understanding before starting to reconcile each stage of the accounting system to each other.

In this chapter we will reconcile the trade receivables control account to the sales ledger and the trade payables control account to the purchase ledger. The control accounts should always reconcile to their appropriate ledger. If they do not there is an error in the accounting system which will require correction. The supplier statement and remittance advices give an indication where there may be errors (but the supplier or customer may be incorrect rather than our system).

An advantage of a digital system is that the sales and purchase ledgers will always reconcile to their respective control accounts because the computer will not make transposition errors. The posting may be wrong (i.e. different amounts to the invoice) but it will still add correctly.

7.1 Reconciliation of Trade Receivables Control Account and Sales Ledger

Periodically the Trade Receivables Control Account (which could be called the Sales Ledger Control Account) and Sales Ledger are reconciled to ensure that they equal each other (reconcile). If there is a difference there is an error.

In real life this would require a review of the postings from the day books into the sales ledger control account and sales ledger to review where the discrepancy occurred. In an exam situation an error will be presented with potential scenarios that could have created that error being provided. You must pick the right answer. To answer this type of exam question

Step 1 total the Trade Receivables Control Account and sales ledger to determine the difference. Note often the sales ledger will include one account with a credit balance to see if debit and credit balances are understood.

Step 2 using the scenario offered create the journal that would have created an error. For example, a £400 invoice being posted once to the sales ledger control account and twice to the sales ledger

Dr Sales ledger control account £400	Cr Sales £400
Dr Sales Ledger £800	

Step 3 reverse this journal from the sales ledger control account and sales ledger

Step 4 if the Trade Receivables Control Account and sales ledger now equal each other after the original journal has been reversed this scenario created the error. If not, it is another scenario.

Alternatively, you will be given an error that has happened and be required to explain the difference. In this situation:

Step 1 set out the journal that has happened, for example posting a sale twice

Step 2 determine which of the options is possible given the journals actually posted rather than those that should have been posted.

You may be given actual figures to determine which is the correct error for each question approach but sometimes you will not be given figures but only words and asked which scenario has the potential to be the cause of the error. In this situation allocate a small amount (say £100) as the difference and the amounts being posted which will turn a theoretical scenario into actual numbers you can use to check your work.

Example:

ABC Ltd has reconciled its Trade Receivables Control Account to its Sales Ledger. The amounts are as follows:

Amount per Trade Receivables Control Account	Amount per Sales Ledger
£100,000 debit	£98,000 debit

Which of the following scenarios could be responsible for the difference:

Posting a sales invoice incorrectly twice to an account in the sales ledger
Posting a discount allowed incorrectly twice to an account in the sales ledger
Posting a sales invoice incorrectly twice to the Trade Receivables Control Account
Posting a discount allowed incorrectly twice to the Trade Receivables Control Account

Step 1: the difference between the Trade Receivables Control Account and the Sales ledger is £2,000 with a journal that has resulted in the sales ledger being £2,000 less than the control account.

Step 2 Create the journal that would create the error

Posting a sales invoice incorrectly twice to an account in the sales ledger	Dr £4,000 to sales ledger Dr £2,000 to the control account
Posting a discount allowed incorrectly twice to an account in the sales ledger	Cr £4,000 to the sales ledger Cr £2,000 to the control account
Posting a sales invoice incorrectly twice to the Trade Receivables Control Account	Dr £4,000 to the control account Dr £2,000 to the sales ledger
Posting a discount allowed incorrectly twice to the Trade Receivables Control Account	Cr £4,000 to the control account Cr £2,000 to the sales ledger

Step 3 and 4 reverse the journal and see if the amounts now reconcile:

		Control account	Sales Ledger
Posting a sales invoice incorrectly twice to an account in the sales ledger	Cr £4,000 to sales ledger Cr £2,000 to the control account	98,000	94,000
Posting a discount allowed incorrectly twice to an account in the sales ledger	Dr £4,000 to the sales ledger Dr £2,000 to the control account	102,000	102,000
Posting a sales invoice incorrectly twice to the Trade Receivables Control Account	Cr £4,000 to the control account Cr £2,000 to the sales ledger	96,000	96,000
Posting a discount allowed incorrectly twice to the Trade Receivables Control Account	Dr £4,000 to the control account Dr £2,000 to the sales ledger	104,000	100,000

If the control account and the ledger reconcile they are the correct options as correcting those journals (reversing them) will bring the Trade Receivables Control Account and Sales Ledger back into balance with each other.

7.2 Reconciliation of Trade Payables Control Account and Purchases Ledger

Periodically the Trade Payables Control Account and Purchases Ledger are reconciled to ensure that they equal each other, which they should do always. If there is a difference in a manual system this is an error.

The steps to correct the error or select the scenario which created the error in the exam is the same as with sales above:

Step 1 total the trade payables control account and purchases ledger to determine the difference. Note often the purchases ledger will include one account with a credit balance to see if debit and credit balances are understood.

Step 2 using the scenario offered create the journal that would have created an error. For example, a £400 invoice being posted once to the purchases ledger control account and twice to the purchases ledger

Cr Purchases ledger control account £400

Cr Purchases Ledger £800

Step 3 reverse this journal from the purchases ledger control account and purchases ledger

Step 4 if the trade payables control account and purchases ledger now equal each other this scenario created the error. If not it is another scenario.

7.3 Trade Receivables and Trade Payables Control T Account Questions

In addition to a reconciliation question between the Trade Receivables/Payables control account and the sales/purchase ledger you may also be given a series of transactions and be asked to produce the T account for the control account.

This is a simple T account question (which is why you must learn double entry bookkeeping using the money in money out method using T accounts) and if you are finding difficulty with it you should revisit chapters 1-5 of the Introduction to Bookkeeping book and repeats the posting from daybooks that you will have seen in that unit.

Note it is possible that the examiner may use interchangeable words for the same thing:

Owed from customers	Trade receivables control account	Sales Ledger control account	Trade debtors control account
Owed to suppliers	Trade payables control account	Purchase Ledger control account	Trade creditors control account

Example:

The following transactions occurred in September. Record the transactions in the Trade Payables Control Account and show the balance carried down.

Balance bfwd	13457
Purchases	12702
Purchases returns	1818
Discounts received	1554
Payments	15246

Purchases returns	1818	Balance bfwd	13457
Discounts received	1554	Purchases	12702
Payments	15246		
Balance cfwd	7541		
Total	26159	Total	26159

The daybooks are posted as follows to the Trade Receivables and Trade Payable Control Accounts:

Trade Receivables Control Account

Debit	Credit
Bfwd	Discounts allowed daybook
Sales daybook	Sales Returns daybook
	Payments (cashbook)
	Irrecoverable debt (Journal)
	Cfwd (typically)

Trade Payables Control Account

Debit	Credit
Discounts received daybook	Bfwd
Purchase Returns daybook	Purchase daybook
Payments (cashbook)	
Cfwd (typically)	

Confirmation of Learning

The Trade Receivables Control Account is reconciled to which ledger? Sales/Purchase

The Trade Payables Control Account is reconciled to which ledger? Sales/Purchase

The control account will always reconcile to its corresponding ledger? True/False

Sales ledger account balances must always be debits? True/False

Question 1

The following accounts have been extracted from the Purchase ledger for ABC Ltd

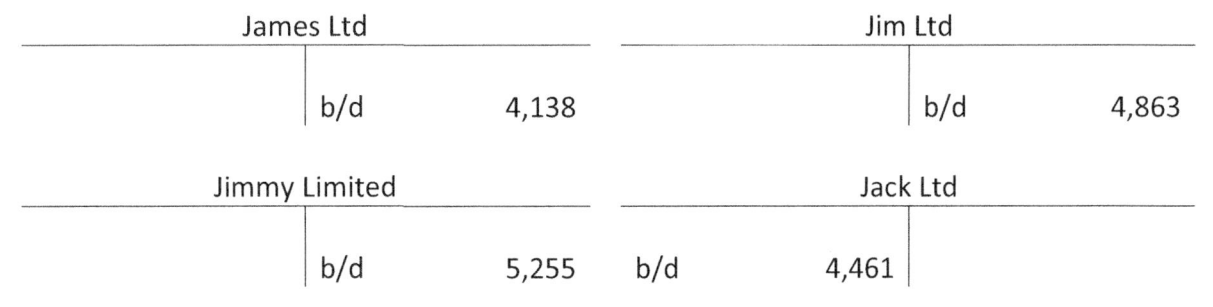

James Ltd			Jim Ltd		
	b/d	4,460		b/d	4,602

Jimmy Limited			Jack Ltd		
	b/d	5,987		b/d	5,644

The following balances have been extracted from the general ledger.

	Debit	Credit
Trade receivables	8,523	
Trade payables		8,523

Which of the following errors is responsible for the failure to reconcile the control account?

Posting an invoice incorrectly twice to the purchase ledger for £882

Posting an invoice incorrectly twice to the purchase ledger for £538

Posting a discount received incorrectly twice to the purchase ledger for £853

Posting a discount received incorrectly twice to the purchase ledger for £710

Question 2

The following accounts have been extracted from the Purchase ledger for ABC Ltd

James Ltd			Jim Ltd		
	b/d	4,138		b/d	4,863

Jimmy Limited			Jack Ltd		
	b/d	5,255	b/d	4,461	

The following balances have been extracted from the general ledger.

	Debit	Credit
Trade receivables	10,506	
Trade payables		10,506

Which of the following errors is responsible for the failure to reconcile the control account?

Posting an invoice incorrectly twice to the purchase ledger for £621

Posting an invoice incorrectly twice to the purchase ledger for £871

Posting a discount received incorrectly twice to the purchase ledger for £711

Posting a discount received incorrectly twice to the purchase ledger for £825

Question 3

The following transactions occurred in January. Record the transactions in the Trade Payables Control Account and show the balance carried down.

Balance bfwd	19869
Purchases	14974
Purchases returns	1641
Discounts received	1173
Payments	19725

Trade Payables Control Account

Bridge to the next chapter

In the next chapter we will revisit the journal to review the types of journals you may be required to post to this daybook in the exam.

Chapter 8 The Journal and Postings to the Daybook

> **Key Points**
>
> The Journal is a daybook for preparing and recording low volume journals.
>
> At level 2 this will be:
>
> 1 Opening balances when starting a company;
>
> 2 Irrecoverable debts; and
>
> 3 Correction of errors and suspense accounts.
>
> 4 Anything that would not go into the other books of prime entry (daybooks) that were considered in the Introduction to Bookkeeping unit.
>
> The preparation of suspense account journals and clearing the suspense T account will form a high number of available marks in the exam. You should refresh your knowledge on daybooks, journals and T accounts from the Introduction to Bookkeeping unit if you do not feel comfortable with these calculations.

In Chapter 5 The Journal daybook was introduced as a daybook where non volume journals would be posted. In this chapter we will consider the types of journals in this unit's exam that are posted to The Journal and how you will create the journals.

The types of journal that are created for posting to The Journal are:

Level 2	Level 3
Opening balance when starting a company	Depreciation
Irrecoverable debts	Accounting for inventories
Correction of errors and suspense accounts	Providing for doubtful debts
	Profit or loss on disposal of non-current assets

This book will consider the adjustments that will be undertaken in the level 2 exam. A question may ask:

Which of the following entries would be entered into The Journal? The answer is whatever journal would not be entered into:

Sales	Sales Daybook	Sales Returns Daybook
Purchases	Purchases Daybook	Purchase Returns Daybook
Discounts	Discounts Allowed daybook	Discounts Received Daybook
Bank Account and Cash	Debit side of cashbook (potentially two column cashbook)	Credit side of cashbook (potentially two column cashbook)
Petty cash expense	Debit side of petty cashbook	Credit side of petty cashbook

The entries into The Journal are set out as journals, rather than totals, that are then posted to the general ledger accounts. Note that this journal could then be posted to the cashbook if it is the ledger account as well as the daybook.

A journal looks like the following in the exam:

Account name	Debit amount	Credit account
Bank	100	
Suspense		100

Students sometimes worry that the debit item should be first. In a manual system in the workplace the journal would actually look like:

Journal number	Date	Account	Debit amount	Credit account
1	31/10/22	Bank	100	
		Suspense		100
		Total	100	100
Being:	Correcting single sided error - reversing journal XXX			

With the credit account indented slightly (which makes it a bit easier to post the journal to the correct side of the account because the indention differentiates between debits and credits reducing transposition errors). The debit balance was traditionally first because it allowed the account name to be lined up more effectively for the indentation of the credit account name (remember this was being written by hand and neatness was vital).

However the AAT exam:

1) Does not indent the detail as it would have been done in the workplace;
2) Does not total the journal (although this should be done and reduces errors).

So it would be harsh if there were marks removed for starting with the credit balance (as no one sees the answers to the exam it is impossible to truly know how the scoring works). However, you are safer to start with the debit balance.

8.1 Opening balance when starting a company

A scenario will be presented for someone starting a company. The journal to be entered into The Journal will be requested. The owner will bring along a series of assets and liabilities with the net amount being their investment (shareholder funds) to maintain the Accounting Equation

$$\text{Assets} = \text{Liabilities} + \text{Capital}$$

The journal will be similar to the trial balance question in Introduction to Bookkeeping where account balances were put into a debit or credit column (only here it is a journal being prepared rather than the trial balance).

Example

Mary Jones is opening up her own business. She brings the following assets into the business at the start of trading.

Item	Value (£'s)
A computer	920
Office furniture	1653
Kettle, microwave and fridge	85
A van	5260
Bank overdraft	633
Trade receivables	774
Trade payables	679

The journal will convert the above into debits and credits with the difference between the two being the amount of shareholder funds:

	Debit	Credit
A computer	920	
Office furniture	1653	
Kettle, microwave and fridge	85	
A van	5260	
Bank overdraft		633
Trade receivables	774	
Trade payables		679
Shareholder funds		7380
Total	8692	8692

8.2 Irrecoverable Debts

An irrecoverable debt is one where a customer has gone into administration whilst owing us money. As a result, due to the limitations of liability we are unlikely to be able to receive this amount. In practice it is possible that a small amount may be recoverable but the exam will typically say that the amount of debt which will be written off (being written down to zero).

The debt no longer has an value so will be written to zero. Therefore

Credit Trade Receivables the amount of the debt.

The debits will be:

1) Any VAT that was due on this debt that would have otherwise been paid to HMRC. This will no longer be payable and is reduction in a money out item and a debit
2) Anything left over will be debit irrecoverable debt expense.

Example:

ABC Ltd has been placed into administration and a debt of £120 can no longer be recovered. VAT is 20% what is the journal to record this transaction?

Dr VAT £20 (the amount of VAT we no longer have to pay to HMRC)

Dr Irrecoverable expense £100 (the amount of the debt lost after deducting the VAT)

Cr Trade Receivables Control Account £120 (the amount of debt being reduced to zero).

ABC Ltd's £120 debtor in the Sales Ledger will also be written to zero through crediting their account £120 (so the Trade receivables control account remains the same as the sales ledger).

8.3 Suspense Accounts

In chapter 5 suspense accounts were introduced where the total of debits did not equal the total of credits in a trial balance. This is because at some point a journal has been entered into the general ledger whose debits did not equal credits (unlike some other errors noted in chapter 4 which did not affect the trial balance tallying).

Suspense account questions will form a large part of the exam (20+ marks) and in this section we will review answering those questions in detail.

8.3.1 Creation of a suspense account journal

When a suspense account is created it is because the debits and credits of a journal in our accounting system do not equal one another. The suspense account is created for the difference for example:

	Debit	Credit
Sales		1000
VAT		200
Trade receivables	1000	
Total	1000	1200

Which would lead to a need for a suspense account of debit £200. This is a one sided journal posted through The Journal (you will not post this as the question will say "a suspense account has been created" meaning this journal has already been posted to the accounts).

When we find the error journal it will need to be reversed which will be a reversal of the error journal plus a posting to the suspense account for the difference:

	Debit	Credit
Sales	1000	
VAT	200	
Trade receivables		1000
Suspense		200
Total	1200	1200

By reversing the journal and posting the difference in the journal to the suspense account we clear the amount we put in the suspense account moving it to zero. This may be asked for as above or as two journals:

Removal of the initial journal:

	Debit	Credit
Sales	1000	
VAT	200	
Trade receivables		1000
Total	1200	1000

Journal to clear the suspense account

	Debit	Credit
Suspense		200
Total	0	200

The totals of the journal are unlikely to be asked for in the exam although they would be used in the workplace as a check whether the addition is correct. Your workings should follow the approach used in the workplace and always total your journals to ensure you do not make a mistake.

The correct journal will then be posted:

	Debit	Credit
Sales		1000
VAT		200
Trade receivables	1200	
Total	1200	1200

Because there a so many entries for a relatively small transaction the correction of suspense accounts generates a lot of marks in the exam. It is however, a very good test of:

1) Double entry bookkeeping
2) VAT

8.3.2 Suspense T account

We may have more than one error affecting the trial balance in our accounting system. In this instance the suspense account balance will be made up of the suspense balance from two or more journals. You may be given these journals and be required to post the suspense journals to the suspense T account to clear it. You might also be asked to update the T account for the other accounts related to the journal or update the account balances in a trial balance.

Example: Journal entries have been updated to correct errors as follows:

	Debit	Credit

Motor vehicle expenses	1578	
Suspense		1578
Suspense	1977	
Motor vehicle expenses		1977

Update the following accounts

Motor vehicle expenses

bal b/d	1842		
Payments	949	Suspense	1977
Suspense	1578	bal c/d	2392
Total	4369	Total	4369

Suspense

		bal b/d	399
Motor vehicle expenses	1977	Motor vehicle expenses	1578
bal c/d	0		
Total	1977	Total	1977

As set out in the Introduction to Bookkeeping unit the description is the account on the other side of the journal (in the workplace it would be the journal number as well because there would be more than one account on the other side of the journal).

Confirmation of Learning

The Journal is used to post low/high volume items to the ledgers.

The assets, liabilities and share capital would be posted via which daybook?

Once all errors have been corrected the balance on the suspense account will be?

Bridge to the next chapter

In the next chapter we will undertake the VAT question which is typically requires preparing a T account from daybook entries or updating due to error corrections. Like all of the questions in this unit (and Introduction to Bookkeeping) your workings should use T accounts wherever possible to reduce the chance of making mistakes.

Questions

Question 1

Which two transactions would be posted to the journal?

Transaction	Daybook
Correcting an error to clear the suspense account	
Posting items to reflect transactions in the bank statement that are not in the ledger account for Bank	
Payment of small expenses	
Journal to record the opening assets and liabilities of a business	
Purchases of amounts from suppliers on credit	

Question 2

Fred Smith is opening up his own business. He brings the following assets into the business at the start of trading.

Item	Value (£'s)
Gardening tools	893
Office furniture	1497
Kettle, microwave and fridge	101
A van	6630
Bank account	1222
Trade receivables	788
Trade payables	892

Complete the opening journal for the business

	Debit	Credit
Gardening tools		
Office furniture		
Kettle, microwave and fridge		
A van		
Bank account		
Trade receivables		
Trade payables		
Shareholder funds		
Total		

Question 3

A sales invoice for £2400 has been posted in full to the Trade Receivables Control account. However only the net has been posted to sales and VAT has been omitted. A suspense account has been created for the difference.

The suspense account value will be

	Debit	Credit
Suspense		

The journal to clear the journal in error will be

	Debit	Credit
Sales		
Trade receivables		

The journal to clear the suspense account will be

	Debit	Credit
Suspense		

The correct journal entry will be

	Debit	Credit
Trade receivables		
Sales		
VAT		

Question 4

Journal entries have been updated to correct errors as follows:

	Debit	Credit
Office furniture	979	
Suspense		979
Suspense	1522	
Office furniture		1522

Update the following accounts

Office furniture

bal b/d	503		
Payments	1432		
Total		Total	

Suspense

		bal b/d	543
Total		Total	

Chapter 9 VAT Control Account

> **Key Points**
>
> The VAT Control Account contains the movements in the amounts due to and from HMRC for VAT taxation.
>
> The amounts are posted to the control account from each of the daybooks (including The Journal where appropriate).
>
> A strong knowledge of T accounts and Daybooks is required for this question. Revisit Introduction to Bookkeeping if required.

VAT is a tax upon sales which is payable by customers on the net amount sold. It is charged to the customer by the supplier who collects the tax and pays it to Her Majesty's Customs & Excise (HMRC). You will most often see the abbreviation HMRC which is the UK government's tax collection agency.

VAT on purchases (provided they are not the end customer for the goods – the member of the general public) can be reclaimed by companies and set off against any amounts due on sales or may even mean that HMRC is paying the company. For a detailed understanding of VAT see the Introduction to Bookkeeping unit.

9.1 Daybooks

The daybooks set out in the Introduction to Bookkeeping unit will include amounts for VAT to be posted to the debit or credit side of the VAT control account. The exam will refer to the various daybooks and expect an understanding of whether the transaction increases the liability to HMRC (which would be a credit in the VAT control account) or reduces the liability to HMRC even to the point of creating a debtor (which would be a debit in the VAT control account).

The daybooks are as follows:

Daybook	Type of VAT	Money flow in VAT control account
Sales	VAT amounts due to HMRC on sales	Increase in liability – credit
Sales returns	VAT that is no longer due to HMRC on sales because the item(s) have been returned	Reduction in liability - debit
Discounts allowed	VAT that is no longer due to HMRC on sales because the amount to be paid for the item(s) has been reduced	Reduction in liability - debit
Purchases	VAT to be reclaimed from HMRC on purchases	Reduction in liability - debit
Purchase returns	VAT that can no longer be reclaimed from HMRC because the items have been returned	Increase in liability – credit
Discounts received	VAT that can no longer be reclaimed from HMRC because the amount due has been	Increase in liability – credit

	reduced	
Debit side of cashbook	VAT amounts due to HMRC on cash sales and amounts received from HMRC for VAT paid	Increase in liability – credit
Credit side of cashbook	VAT amounts due from HMRC on cash purchases and amounts paid to HMRC for VAT liabilities	Reduction in liability - debit
Debit side of petty cashbook	VAT amounts due to HMRC on cash sales	Increase in liability – credit
Credit side of petty cashbook	VAT amounts due from HMRC on cash purchases	Reduction in liability - debit
The Journal	Irrecoverable debts reduce the amount due from customers and the amount to be paid to HMRC	Reduction in liability - debit
The Journal	Correction of errors	Could be either debits or credits

9.2 The T Account

The T account for the VAT control account would therefore look like:

VAT Control Account

Sales Returns Daybook	Sales Daybook
Discounts Allowed Daybook	
Purchases Daybook	Purchase Returns Daybook
	Discounts Received Daybook
Credit side of Cashbook	Debit side of Cashbook
Credit side of Petty Cashbook	Debit side of Petty Cashbook
The Journal – Irrecoverable debts	

The Journal correction of errors could be either side

Bridge to the Next Chapter

In the next chapter we will look at a control account that is designed to ensure the posting of wages expenses is accurate – the Wages Control Account.

Confirmation of learning

A transaction that increases the liability due to HMRC is a debit/credit in the VAT control account? True/False?

VAT on purchases increases/decreases the liability due to HMRC? True/False?

Payments can only be made to HMRC. HMRC will not pay monies to the company. True/False?

Question 1

ABC Ltd has the following entries for VAT from its daybooks in its control account. Which side of the VAT control account will the entries be posted?

	Amount	Debit	Credit
VAT on cash sales in the cashbook	1080		1080
Payment from HMRC in cashbook	1025		1025
VAT in the discounts allowed daybook	83	83	
VAT in the discounts received daybook	51		51
VAT in the purchase returns daybook	12		12
VAT on irrecoverable debt	89	89	

Question 2

ABC Ltd has the following entries for VAT from its daybooks in its control account. Which side of the VAT control account will the entries be posted?

	Amount	Debit	Credit
VAT on cash purchases in cashbook	1618	1618	
VAT on cash sales in the cashbook	989		989
HMRC entry in Debit side of cashbook	629		629
VAT in the discounts received daybook	14		14
VAT in the sales returns daybook	78	78	
VAT on cash sales in the petty cashbook	187		187

The balance bfwd on the VAT control account is set out below. What is the balance carried forward after posting the above to the control account?

	Debit	Credit
Balance bfwd	192	
Balance cfwd		69

Chapter 10 Wages Control and Processing Wages Expenses

> **Key Points**
>
> Every wages question has four steps:
>
> Step 1 create the table with 3 main lines in it and put the numbers you have in it
>
> Step 2 fill in the rest of the table with the numbers you have a work out the missing numbers
>
> Step 3 create the journals
>
> Step 4 create the wages control account and check it balances to zero
>
> Then answer the question.
>
> If you follow this approach it is easy to score 100%. If you don't you will typically achieve low marks.

Processing wages expenses and the Wages Control account is a question where students tend to lose most of the easier marks in the exam turning a very easy question into a low scoring question. The reasons for this are:

1) The examiner will only ask for part of the information (similar to bank reconciliations) and in this question it is very tempting to attempt to calculate just part of the overall wages expense independently of the other elements of the overall control;
2) The Wages Control account at first glance appears counterintuitive. Certain elements seem pointless, why bother posting to a Wages Control account when you could just post directly to the various directly.

However, if you complete the full processing of wages (which you are given time to do) for every wages control question this becomes a very easy question.

10.1 Wages Expenses

Wages expenses to the employer are made up of:

1) The salary that is agreed to be paid to the employee by the employer;
2) Additional costs that are incurred by the employer for employing the person. These are:
   a. Employer's National Insurance contributions – a tax on employing people (notionally for expenditure such as NHS, unemployment benefits etc but it is just a tax with some minor complications for state benefits);
   b. Employer's pension contributions – employers are expected to contribute towards an employee's pension for retirement;
   c. Apprenticeship levy – this is unlikely to be included in the exam but in the workplace this is a contribution towards apprenticeship costs in the country and employers can use it to pay for apprenticeship training (or lose it if they do not employ apprentices).

    d. Other costs to be paid by the employer – you will not see these in the exam but in the workplace salary sacrifice schemes may have contributions from the employer in addition to contributions from the employee.

The amount the employer receives will not be the salary that is agreed to be paid to the employee by the employer. The employee will have to pay:

1) Taxes;
    a. Income tax;
    b. Employees National Insurance tax (again as above associated with certain government spending but it is mainly just tax as you do not get preferential treatment in the NHS because you notionally paid for part of it);
2) Employee pension contributions towards their pension in retirement; and
3) Voluntary deductions the employee may choose to contribute towards. These could be:
    a. Trade union contributions for being a member of a trade union (who represents the employee);
    b. Attachments to earnings by court order, for example payments for child support.
    c. In the workplace there will be salary sacrifice schemes to buy certain things which can be used to reduce the employee's tax burden (the employees is provided goods or services by the employer instead of money which in certain circumstances results in tax savings). An example could be the employee sacrifices salary in return for an electric car. This might be too complicated to appear in the exam as an option but is a voluntary deduction (so could).

The employee will receive their net wages paid into their bank account which will be the gross wages (amount agreed to be paid by the employer) less taxation, pension and other deductions.

An exam question will give you some information and from that you are to determine other figures. The examiner will not ask for all of the potential figures in the hope that you omit something in a rush making a mistake. To counter this the start of all Wages Processing/Control questions should be the creation of a table:

Step 1 Create a table with 3 lines and space in between and populate whichever line you have (you will normally only be given one of the three lines at random – i.e. it will not always be the total expense)

	Amount £
Total Wages Expense	100,000
Gross Wages	
Net Wages	

Step 2 Put in the employers expenses above the gross wages and the employees deductions below the gross wages.

		Amount £
	Total Wages Expense	100,000
Paid by employer	Employer's NI	10,000
	Employer's Pension contributions	5,000
	Apprenticeship levy/other employer cost	1,000
	Gross Wages	
Paid by employee	Income tax	10,000
	Employees' NI	2,000
	Employees' pension contributions	5,000
	Trade union subscriptions	1,000
	Other deductions	1,000
	Net Wages	

Step 3 fill in the missing two rows

		Amount £
	Total Wages Expense	100,000
Paid by employer	Employer's NI	10,000
	Employer's Pension contributions	5,000
	Apprenticeship levy/other employer cost	1,000
	Gross Wages	84,000
Paid by employee	Income tax	10,000
	Employees' NI	2,000
	Employees' pension contributions	5,000
	Trade union subscriptions	1,000
	Other deductions	1,000
	Net Wages	65,000

Step 4 Only now answer the question regarding the requested value.

10.2 Paying the Wages Expense – the Wages Control

The Wages Control account is a method by which the total cost of salaries are posted to the general ledger and control accounts that will be used to pay the various payments that must be made. Section 9.1 highlighted a large number of different agencies being paid different amounts (which also have different timings for example employees being paid before the month end but HMRC being paid just after the month end).

The Wages Control is used as a check to ensure the correct journals are created and once all of those transfers to make the payments are made, if the wages control is zero the financial transactions have been posted and made correctly. Unlike the other control accounts shown previously (where there will typically always be a debit or credit balance) the objective of the wages control is to return to a zero balance.

The point of this control account is to assure the senior accountant in the department that the more junior accountants have completed their tasks correctly. If all of the more junior accounts complete their tasks correctly and make the correct payments the wages control returns to zero. The senior accountant now only needs to check the suspense account has a zero balance in it rather than check everyone's work in detail. No professional accountant should ever assume that everyone is working accurately and effectively.

The process of creating the Wages Control is as follows:

Step 1 From the table produced in section 9.1 to create the figures for each line item produce the journals that will post the cost of wages being:

a. Dr Wages expense total wages expense to the employer
   Cr Wages control total wages expense to the employer
b. Dr Wages control employers national insurance
   Cr HMRC taxation creditor account which will be paid later
c. Dr Wages control employers pension contributions
   Cr Pension creditor which will be paid later
d. Dr Wages Control employees national insurance
   Cr HMRC taxation creditor account which will be paid later
e. Dr Wages Control Income tax
   Cr HMRC taxation creditor account which will be paid later
f. Dr Wages Control for pension deductions, trade union subs etc (repeat for each deduction)
   Cr the creditor account for each of the deductions
g. Dr Wages Control for net salaries
   Cr Bank for payment of net salaries

The journals for the processing of wages for the example in section 9.1 would be:

Detail	Debit	Credit
Wages expense	100,000	
Wages control		100,000
HMRC control (ers NI)		10,000
Wages control	10,000	
Pensions control (employers pension contributions)		5,000
Wages control	5,000	
HMRC control (apprenticeship levy)		1,000
Wages control	1,000	
HMRC Control (Income tax)		10,000
Wages control	10,000	
HMRC Control (Employees' NI)		2,000
Wages control	2,000	
Pension control (Employees' pension contributions)		5,000
Wages control	5,000	
Trade union subscriptions control		1,000
Wages control	1,000	
Other deductions control		1,000
Wages control	1,000	
Bank (payment of employees net salary		65,000
Wages control	65,000	
Total	200,000	200,000

Step 2 Post the journals to the T accounts in the general ledger and check that the Wages Control account is zero.

Wages Control

		Wages expense	100,000
HMRC	23,000		
Pensions	10,000		
Trade unions	1,000		
Other control	1,000		
Bank	65,000		
		c/d	0
Total	100,000	Total	100,000

Step 3 Only now answer the question for the journal for the particular item or completion of the Wages Control.

The key method to obtaining high marks in the Wages Control question is to complete steps 1 and 2 first (having already completed the table of costs) before trying to answer the question. The examiner will not ask for every journal but any short-cut taken can lead to elements being missed and the work not being checked effectively (does your Wages Control equal zero?).

You may consider the Wages Control to be a significant waste of time. Why not just post the journals directly through the control accounts/cashbook without so much fuss back and forth? The Wages Control can offer a solution that checks if the journals have been posted correctly to the accounts and provides a solution to the timing difference between the processing of net wages to be paid to the employ and their payment into the bank account.

However in the workplace you would just post:

Detail	Debit	Credit
Wages expense	100,000	
HMRC control (ers NI)		10,000
Pensions control (employers pension contributions)		5,000
HMRC control (apprenticeship levy)		1,000
HMRC Control (Income tax)		10,000
HMRC Control (Employees' NI)		2,000
Pension control (Employees' pension contributions)		5,000
Trade union subscriptions control		1,000
Other deductions control		1,000
Wages Liability Control		65,000
Total	100,000	100,000

And then post

Dr Wages liability control £65,000

Cr Bank £65,000

When the net wages payment is made.

However, by using a Wages Control the examiner offers a lot of easy marks in the exam (provided you do not take any short-cuts).

In total in answering wages questions in the exam we have four steps:

Step 1 create the table with 3 main lines in it and put the numbers you have in it

Step 2 fill in the rest of the table with the numbers you have a work out the missing numbers

Step 3 create the journals

Step 4 create the wages control account and check it balances to zero

Then answer the question.

10.3 Control Accounts vs Suspense Accounts

Control accounts should not be confused with suspense accounts. In real life there may also be holding accounts where an item is being stored because we do not know what it is. For example an unknown item has appeared in the bank account

Dr cash

Cr ?

We could put the credit amount in a holding account and post it when we have for example received a later remittance advice or chase a debtor who tells us they have paid. The journal is then

Dr Holding account

Cr The correct account.

Some examples of Wages Control questions are worked through here:

Wages Control examples of 4 Step method AAT Bookkeeping Controls Level 2 - YouTube

Confirmation of Learning

To save time in the exam you can only answer the part of the question the examiner asks about. True/False

The Wages Control should always balance to zero at the end of the period. True/False

The amount an employer incurs in expenses is only the amount they agree to pay for employees' salaries. True/False

Bridge to the next chapter

The next chapter will be a repeat of the trial balance question that you were asked in the Introduction to Bookkeeping unit. You should be familiar with the question on the Accounting Equation.

Questions

Question 1

ABC Ltd has the following wages expenses for September

	£
Net Wages	77,013
Employers National Insurance	4,783
Employees National Insurance	4,783
Trade Union Contributions	956
Other employee contributions	956
Income tax	25,112
Employees' Pension Contribution	10,762
Employers Pension contribution	7,174

What is the gross wages payable in the month?

	Debit	Credit
Gross wages		

Prepare the Wages Control account for the month:

Wages Control Account

Options

HMRC control account	Trade union control account	Bank
Pension control account	Other employee contribution control account	Wages Expense

Question 2

XYZ Ltd has the following wages expenses for March

	£
Total cost to the employer	93,953
Employees' Pension Contribution	5,925
Employers Pension contribution	5,925
Trade Union Contributions	253
Other employee contributions	846
Income tax	18,621
Employees National Insurance	2,539
Employers National Insurance	3,385

What are the following journals to the Wages Control account?

HMRC
Dr
    Cr

Trade union control
Dr
    Cr

Payment of wages to employees
Dr
    Cr

Options

Wages control account	HMRC control account	Trade union control account	Bank

Note with both of the wages control questions you are only being asked for part of the wages control process in the hope that you will attempt to short-cut the question. However, your answer should cover the full wages control process and then extract the answers from your full workings.

Chapter 11 Extract and Initial Trial Balance and Update the Trial Balance - The Accounting Equation (Repeat from Introduction to Bookkeeping)

> **Key Points**
>
> In the exam you will create/complete/update a trial balance from an extract from the general ledger. This is a repeat of the trial balance question from Introduction to Bookkeeping – with some additional potential to update for errors/reconciliations etc.
>
> We balance off T accounts in order to provide an additional check that the balance of the account has been added correctly
>
> If shareholder reserves is missing from a list of balances for the creation of the opening balance sheet question: shareholder capital is the difference between the debits and credits such that the balance sheet tallies

11.1 Balancing off an account

At the end of an accounting period (a point where reports will be produced from the accounts) the T accounts in the general ledger are "balanced down" for the purposes of determining the amount in each account. To do this:

Step 1: both sides of the T account are totaled. A carried down (sometimes called carried forward) balancing figure is put into the side of the T account that totals the smallest number so that both sides of the T account should add up to the same amount. The balanced down figure is dated at the end of the accounting period.

Step 2: the figures of both sides are recalculated to check the totals of both sides are now the same. This is a check for any miscasting errors (which are very time consuming to fix in a manual system should they appear as the whole set of accounts then has to be recast).

Step 3: the carried down figure becomes a brought down figure on the other side of the T account at the start of the next period. The brought down figure is dated at the start of the next period. The brought down figure is the balance to be used in the trial balance.

Bank

Capital £30,000	Van £10,000
	c/d £20,000
£30,000	£30,000
b/d £20,000	

Van

Bank £10,000	c/d £10,000
£10,000	£10,000
b/d £10,000	

Capital

	Bank £30,000
c/d £30,000	
£30,000	£30,000
	b/d £30,000

Sales

	Trade rec £20,000
c/d £20,000	
£20,000	£20,000
	b/d £20,000

Trade receivables

Sales £20,000	c/d £20,000
£20,000	£20,000
b/d £20,000	

Students sometimes find the concept of the carried down figure strange. Why have it at all when we could simply put the total net figure as the brought down number for the next period as below:

Bank	Van	Capital
Capital £30,000	Van £10,000 Bank £10,000	Bank £30,000
b/d £20,000	b/d £10,000	c/d £30,000

Sales	Trade receivables
Trade rec £20,000	Sales £20,000
b/d £20,000	b/d £20,000

In a digital/computerised accounting system this is exactly what happens. The minuses (credits) are deducted from pluses (credits) to provide an overall balance (plus or minus) for the account.

However, in a manual system it is less prone to error to total both sides, put in the carried down figure and then total them again to ensure that they add up to the same number. It is a check to ensure that the work is correct, and nothing more, but in a manual system this is very important. It is also important in an exam but not required in real life where a digital system is used.

The AAT exam will ask for the dates of the b/d and c/d balances (and will continue to do so in future units). The period end will be given (typically the month end). This will be the date for the c/d balance. The b/d balance date will be the start of the next month. If the month end was 31 October the dates would look like:

Bank

1/10	b/d	5,000			
6/10	Cash sales	2,000	9/10	HMRC VAT	500
			13/10	Purchases	500
			31/10	c/d	6,000
Total		7,000	Total		7,000
1/11	b/d	6,000			

The b/d balance is the amount to be used for the trial balance. The c/d balance is only an additional aid to check that numbers are correctly totaled although the examiner refers to this as a "balance" and "the balance at the end of the period" which confuses students (where does the money come from for this balance is a frequent question). The c/d balance is just a balancing figure to check additions and the balance on the account for the trial balance is the b/d figure.

11.2 The Trial Balance

A total of all of the brought down balances in the general ledger is a trial balance. Because it is based upon two-sided journal entries the total of the debits should always equal the total of the credits (or the positive money should always equal the negative money).

	Debit	**Credit**
Van	£10,000	
Bank	£20,000	
Trade receivables	£20,000	
Sales		£20,000
Shareholder capital		£30,000
Total	£50,000	£50,000

11.3 Creation of a Trial Balance

In the exam:

1) You will be given a list of amounts that you are to convert into a trial balance. In answering this question imagine that you are starting from nothing (all accounts being zero) and creating a journal that would result in the balances set out in the question. What is the type of item (money in or out) what is the direction this amount would create (increasing or decreasing) and this will provide the debit or credit. There are two things to be mindful of:
    a. Be careful to check whether the item is a money in item or a money out item. For example, cash in bank is typically a money in item. However, if it is changed to bank (overdraft) this will be money going out in future. This part of the question is deliberate to determine any learners who are attempting to pass the question using the DEAD CLIC mnemonic (with bank being an asset and always a debit using it);
    b. You may not be given the shareholder funds (capital). This may have to be calculated as the total of

    Assets – Liabilities = Missing share capital figure

    to ensure that the balance sheet tallies.

Capital is made up of the starting capital for the year and movements in year from both financial performance and any receipts/payments from/to shareholders. The financial performance in year will typically be provided (sales, expenses etc) the other changes in capital will be the missing figure and will be the difference between the totals of your list of debits and credits. It is possible for this figure to be a debit (i.e. the company has made losses that exceed shareholder capital paid to the company) although it is unlikely.

2) You will be given a an extracted balance which you are to update for additional accounts or transactions (for example correcting some errors). For this:
   a. The approach for creating the trial balance before adjustments is as per point 1 above;
   b. Create journals for the transactions to be posted. Total the journals and check that the debits equal the credits;
   c. Post the journals to T accounts for the accounts to be updated;
   d. The b/d balances on the updated accounts are the new balances for the adjusted trial balance.

Whilst this takes longer than just updating the accounts for the numbers you think should be updated it will always be correct

Confirmation of Learning

A trial balance is a list of the totals of the accounts in which ledger?

Every account in the trial balance must equal zero [True/False]

If the shareholder capital figure is missing from the opening trial balance question the amount should be entered zero [True/False]

It is the month of July.

The carried down figure for the period is dated [ ]?

The brought down figure for the following period is dated [ ]?

The balance for the trial balance is the amount dated [31 July/1 August]?

If required reinforce your knowledge of chapters 1-5 of the Introduction to Bookkeeping book and undertake the paper and cups method of learning double entry bookkeeping here:

Double Entry Bookkeeping for AAT Level 2 and AAT Level 3 - YouTube

Question 1

On 31 January a partially prepared trial balance had debit balances totalling £163645 and credit balances totalling £198081

The accounts below have not yet been entered into the trial balance. Complete the table below to show whether each balance will be a debit or a credit entry in the trial balance.

	Amount	Debit	Credit
VAT control account (owed by HMRC)	14,080		
Bank account overdraft	15,476		
Share capital	19,378		
Trade receivables control	16,454		

The totals of debits and credits in the completed trial balance are

	Debit	Credit
Totals		

Question 2

On 31 January a partially prepared trial balance had debit balances totalling £139547 and credit balances totalling £149042.

The accounts below have not yet been entered into the trial balance. Complete the table below to show whether each balance will be a debit or a credit entry in the trial balance.

	Amount	Debit	Credit
VAT control account (owed to HMRC)	14,907		
Bank account overdraft	12,399		
Share capital	19,330		
Trade receivables control	17,471		

The totals of debits and credits in the completed trial balance are

	Debit	Credit
Totals		

Following review it is noted that the month's entries from the Sales daybook have not been posted to the account being

	Total	Net	VAT
Sales Daybook Totals	39,276	32,730	6,546

Update the trial balance following correction of this error

	Debit	Credit
Other accounts		
VAT control account (owed to HMRC)		
Bank account overdraft		
Trade receivables control		
Share capital		
Total		

Chapter 12 Conclusion

At this point in your studies you should now understand the subject covered by this unit and practiced a number of exam standard questions. A walkthrough of the AAT practice assessment is provided in the playlist that accompanies this unit. It is recommended that you undertake that walkthrough answering the questions yourself first to the time prescribed and watch the answers (paying close attention to the technique used).

Once you complete that a practice assessment is provided at the end of this book. Together with additional practice assessments you may obtain this will be the correct preparation for the exam.

Thank You and a Request

I hope you enjoyed reading this book as much as I enjoyed writing it. This book has been brought to you via Amazon direct publishing which allows authors like myself to self-publish without the need for a large publishing house. This has provided a book at around 30% of the cost of the large publishers and one which I feel better reflects the needs of the exam. However, it does not have the marketing backing of the large publishers.

If you have felt that this book helped with your studies it would be greatly appreciated if you would spare a moment to leave a review so that it can be marketed to other students like yourself. May I also take this opportunity to wish you good luck with the exam.

Michael

Answers

Chapter 3

Confirmation of Learning

8 days although it could be up to 10 days.

Standing order

Bank draft

Question 1

Situation	Answer
John's Autos wants to be paid in something that is similar to cash but not cash for a car	Bank draft
Tea and coffee required to be purchased from the local shop	Cash
£100 to be paid on the 1st of each month for rental of a garage lock up	Standing order
Variable expenses incurred by a salesperson over the month	Credit card

Question 2

Cheque	Debit card purchase	Bank draft	CHAPS	**Credit card purchase**

Question 3

Approach	Yes/No
To pay late and wait to be chased before payment	No
To pay as late as possible but not late	Yes
To pay a supplier late because they cannot complain about it	No
To pay immediately to clear the creditor from the accounts	No

Chapter 4

Confirmation of learning

4 steps to a bank reconciliation

Step 1 – tick the cashbook to the bank statement;

Step 2 - reconcile the opening balances

Step 3 - adjust the cashbook

Step 4 - reconcile the bank statement to the adjusted cash book

No step can be missed in the exam even if the exam question suggests it can. By completing the full bank reconciliation you will have 100% confidence you are correct.

Question 1: Note how this question only asks for part of the 4 step process (reconcile the brought forward balances) however you should always do the full bank reconciliation (there will be another part asking for something else in any cash so you should not be fooled by this).

Previous months bank reconciliation

Balance per bank statement		-973
Add outstanding lodgements		
Invoice X523504	78	
Total		78
Less unpresented cheques		
FrontMax Windows	-94	
		-94
Balance per cashbook		-989

Updated Cashbook

					bfwd	904
02/03/22	Invoice X523511		41	21/03/22	LovelyAmazon	98
31/03/22	cfwd		961			
	Total		2263		Total	2263
				01/04/22	bfwd	961

Bank Reconciliation

Balance per bank statement		-908
Add outstanding lodgements		
Total		0
Less unpresented cheques		
Moments Count	-53	
		-53
Balance per cashbook		-961

Chapter 5

> **Confirmation of Learning**
>
> If the debits and the credits in the trial balance equal one another our accounting system is free from errors. False
>
> For the debits and credits in the trial balance to not equal each other the journal(s) that led to the error must have debits that do not equal credits. True
>
> If an accounting system finds an error whose debits do not equal credits the trial balance must not be in balance. False – There could be a compensating error

Question 1

Assign the correct classification to the following errors:

Error	Classification
Two or more errors occur whose debits do not equal credits but their effect on the trial balance cancel each other out	Compensating Errors
A loan repayment is credited to payment of shareholder capital	Error of Principle
£600 payment by A Jones Plumbers is credited to A Johns Ltd in the sales ledger	Error of Commission
The Sales Daybook is posted to the general ledger as Debit Sales £1000 Debit VAT £200 Credit Sales Ledger Control Account £1200	Reversal of Entries

Question 2

Which of the following errors cause the trial balance to no longer balance?

Error	Will cause and imbalance in the trial balance (Yes/No)
A cash purchase is posted to the purchases and VAT accounts only	Yes
A purchase of a motor vehicle has been posted to the motor expense account instead. All other entries are correct.	No
A customer receipt was debited to the sales ledger control account and credited to the bank account	No
A petty cash expense for £15 was posted as £51 to the analysis column in the petty cash book but as £15 in the total column.	Yes

Chapter 6

> **Confirmation of learning**
>
> True
>
> How is the suspense account cleared? By reversing the incorrect journals with the suspense account entries being the difference in the incorrect journal between the debits and credits
>
> The Journal

Question 1

What amount will be in the suspense account before these journals are corrected?

	Dr	Cr
Suspense	£900	

What is the total of debits and credits after the suspense account is created?

	Dr	Cr
Total of trial balance	£100,900	100,900

Question 2

A suspense account should be created for:

	Dr	Cr
Suspense	£2,000	

Correcting which of the following errors would clear the suspense account:

Error	Would help clear	Would not help clear
An error omitting a sales invoice from the sales daybook		Would not help clear
A single sided entry in a journal	Would help clear	
An error of commission		Would not help clear
An error where VAT on a purchase had been incorrectly entered into the daybook as £120 rather than £210. All other entries being correct.	Would help clear	

Chapter 7

Confirmation of Learning

The Trade Receivables Control Account is reconciled to which ledger? Sales

The Trade Payables Control Account is reconciled to which ledger? Purchase

The control account will always reconcile to its corresponding ledger? False – it should always reconcile but there could be an error

Sales ledger account balances must always be debits? False – customers may pay in advance, overpay, or receive a credit.

Question 1

	Debit	Credit
Total of purchase ledger		9,405
Total of Trade Payables Control Account		8,523
Difference		882

Impact of journal posted on purchase ledger	Debit	Credit	Purchase ledger when reversed
Posting an invoice incorrectly twice to the purchase ledger for £882		882	8,523
Posting an invoice incorrectly twice to the purchase ledger for £538		538	7,985
Posting a discount received incorrectly twice to the purchase ledger for £853	853		10,258
Posting a discount received incorrectly twice to the purchase ledger for £710	710		9,233

Question 2

	Debit	Credit
Total of purchase ledger		9,795
Total of Trade Payables Control Account		10,506
Difference	711	

Impact of journal posted on purchase ledger	Debit	Credit	Purchase ledger when reversed
Posting an invoice incorrectly twice to the purchase ledger for £621		621	9,174
Posting an invoice incorrectly twice to the purchase ledger for £871		871	9,635
Posting a discount received incorrectly twice to the purchase ledger for £711	711		10,506
Posting a discount received incorrectly twice to the purchase ledger for £825	825		11,331

Question 3

Purchases returns	1641	Balance bfwd	19869
Discounts received	1173	Purchases	14974
Payments	19725		
Balance cfwd	12304		
Total	34843	Total	34843

Chapter 8

Confirmation of Learning

The Journal is used to post low volume items to the ledgers.

The assets, liabilities and share capital would be posted via which daybook? The Journal

Once all errors have been corrected the balance on the suspense account will be zero.

Question 1

Which two transactions would be posted to the journal?

Transaction	Daybook
Correcting an error to clear the suspense account	The Journal
Posting items to reflect transactions in the bank statement that are not in the ledger account for Bank	Cashbook
Payment of small expenses	Petty Cashbook
Journal to record the opening assets and liabilities of a business	The Journal
Purchases of amounts from suppliers on credit	Purchase daybook

Question 2

	Debit	Credit
Gardening tools	893	
Office furniture	1497	
Kettle, microwave and fridge	101	
A van	6630	
Bank account	1222	
Trade receivables	788	
Trade payables		892
Shareholder funds		10239
Total	11131	11131

Question 3

The suspense account value will be

	Debit	Credit
Suspense		400

The journal to clear the journal in error will be

	Debit	Credit
Sales	2000	
Trade receivables		2400

The journal to clear the suspense account will be

	Debit	Credit
Suspense	400	

The correct journal entry will be

	Debit	Credit
Trade receivables	2400	
Sales		2000
VAT		400

Question 4

Office furniture

bal b/d	503		
Payments	1432	Suspense	1522
Suspense	979	bal c/d	1392
Total	2914	Total	2914

Suspense

		bal b/d	543
Office furniture	1522	Office furniture	979
bal c/d	0		
Total	1522	Total	1522

Chapter 9

Confirmation of learning

True

True

False

Question 1

	Amount	Debit	Credit
VAT on cash sales in the cashbook	1080		1080
Payment from HMRC in cashbook	1025		1025
VAT in the discounts allowed daybook	83	83	
VAT in the discounts received daybook	51		51
VAT in the purchase returns daybook	12		12
VAT on irrecoverable debt	89	89	

Question 2

	Amount	Debit	Credit
VAT on cash purchases in cashbook	1618	1618	
VAT on cash sales in the cashbook	989		989
HMRC entry in Debit side of cashbook	629		629
VAT in the discounts received daybook	14		14
VAT in the sales returns daybook	78	78	
VAT on cash sales in the petty cashbook	187		187

	Debit	Credit
Balance bfwd	192	
Balance cfwd		69

VAT Control Account

b/d	192			
VAT on cash purchases in cashbook	1618			
		VAT on cash sales in the cashbook	989	
		HMRC entry in Debit side of cashbook	629	
		VAT in the discounts received daybook	14	
VAT in the sales returns daybook	78			
		VAT on cash sales in the petty cashbook	187	
		c/d	69	
Total	1888	Total	1888	

Chapter 10

Confirmation of Learning

False – you will only be asked for part of the wages control process to see if you will take short cuts and make a mistake

True

False they also have employment tax and expenses

Question 1

Total cost to the employer	131,539
Employers Pension contribution	7,174
Employers National Insurance	4,783
Gross pay	119,582
Income tax	25,112
Employees National Insurance	4,783
Employees Pension Contribution	10,762
Trade Union Contributions	956
Other employee contributions	956
Net Wages	77,013

			£	£
Dr	Wages Expense		131,539	
	Cr	Wages control account		131,539
Dr	Wages control account		34,678	
	Cr	HMRC control account		34,678
Dr	Wages control account		17,936	
	Cr	Pension control account		17,936
Dr	Wages control account		956	
	Cr	Trade union control account		956
Dr	Wages control account		956	
	Cr	Other employee contribution control account		956
Dr	Wages control account		77,013	
	Cr	Bank		77,013

Wages Control Account

HMRC control account	34,678	Wages Expense	131,539
Pension control account	17,936		
Trade union control account	956		
Other employee contribution control account	956		
Bank	77,013		
	131,539		131,539

Question 2

Total cost to the employer	93,953
Employers Pension contribution	5,925
Employers National Insurance	3,385
Gross pay	84,643
Income tax	18,621
Employees National Insurance	2,539
Employees Pension Contribution	5,925
Trade Union Contributions	253
Other employee contributions	846
Net Wages	56,459

				£	£
Dr	Wages Expense			93,953	
	Cr	Wages control account			93,953
Dr	Wages control account			24,545	
	Cr	HMRC control account			24,545
Dr	Wages control account			11,850	
	Cr	Pension control account			11,850
Dr	Wages control account			253	
	Cr	Trade union control account			253
Dr	Wages control account			846	
	Cr	Other employee contribution control account			846
Dr	Wages control account			56,459	
	Cr	Bank			56,459

Wages Control Account

HMRC control account	24,545	Wages Expense	93,953
Pension control account	11,850		
Trade union control account	253		
Other employee contribution control account	846		
Bank	56,459		
	93,953		93,953

Chapter 11

Confirmation of Learning

A trial balance is a list of the totals of the accounts in which ledger? General ledger

Every account in the trial balance must equal zero False

If the shareholder capital figure is missing from the opening trial balance question the amount should be entered zero False – it is the difference between the debits and credits

It is the month of July.

The carried down figure for the period is dated 31 July

The brought down figure for the following period is dated 1 August

The balance for the trial balance is the amount dated 1 August

Question 1

	Amount	Debit	Credit
VAT control account (owed by HMRC)	14,080	14,080	
Bank account overdraft	15,476		15,476
Share capital	19,378	19,378	
Trade receivables control	16,454	16,454	

	Debit	Credit
Totals	213,557	213,557

Question 2

	Amount	Debit	Credit
VAT control account (owed to HMRC)	14,907		14,907
Bank account overdraft	12,399		12,399
Share capital	19,330	19,330	
Trade receivables control	17,471	17,471	

	Debit	Credit
Totals	176,348	176,348

	Debit	Credit
Other accounts	139,547	149,042
VAT control account (owed to HMRC)		21,453
Bank account overdraft		12,399
Trade receivables control	56,747	
Share capital		13,400
Total	196,294	196,294

Index

Bank reconciliations	26-37
Bank statements	26-30
Debits and Credits	8
Five stage accounting system	12
Journal Daybook, The Journal	46, 56-64
Irrecoverable Debts	58
Opening balance journal when starting a company	57
Payment methods	18
BACS	22
Bank draft	20
Cash or petty cash	18
CHAPS	22
Charge card or supplier card	21
Cheques	19
Credit card	21
Debit card	20
Direct credit	24
Direct debit	23
Faster payments	22
Mobile banking/bank transfers	23
Standing orders	23
Treasury Management	24
Suspense Accounts	43, 59
Suspense T account	60
T Accounts	9
Trade Payables Control account	49-56
Reconciliation of Trade Payables Control Account and Purchases Ledger	52
Trade Receivables and Trade Payables Control T Account Questions	52
Trade Receivables Control Account	49-56
Reconciliation of Trade Receivables Control Account and Sales Ledger	49
Trial Balance	76-82
Balancing off an account	76
Creation of a Trial Balance	78
Updating a Trial Balance	79
Types of Error	37-43
Compensating Error	40
Error of Commission	39
Error of Omission	38
Error of Original Entry	39
Error of Principle	38
Error of reversal	39
Extracting of Trial Balance Error	40
Miscasting error	40
Single Sided Errors or Two Errors on the Same Side of the Journal	40
Transposition Error and Different Credits and Debits	40

VAT	11
Daybooks posting to VAT control account	64
VAT Control Account	64
VAT T account	65
Wages Control Account	67-75
Paying the Wages Expense – the Wages Control	70
Wages Expenses	67

Free practice assessment

The following practice assessment is 100 marks which should be completed with 1.5 hours.

Task 1 (10 Marks)

(a) Match the most appropriate payment method to the situation

Situation	Answer	Potential Payment Methods	
Payment sent through post		Faster payments	Cash
Reimbursement of small expenses for a meeting		Credit card	Supplier card
Variable payment at the end of each month for electricity		Cheque	BACS
Fuel expenses for a fleet of vehicles all using the same franchise of garages		Bank draft	Direct Debit

4 Marks

(b) Which two of the following will not reduce funds in the account on the date of payment/put in post.

Debit card purchase	Supplier card	Faster Payments	BACS	Cheque

2 Marks

(c) Jane's Plumbers has a big payment coming into the business a 30 April 2022 but a short-term cashflow issue until then. Which order should the following suppliers be paid (1 being first and 4 being last)

ABC Ltd	£2000 invoice dated 12 April 2022 – terms net monthly	
XYZ plc	£2000 invoice dated 12 April 2022 – terms 2% discount if paid within 7 days, payment due within 14 days	
OBO LLP	£2000 invoice dated 12 April 2022 – terms payment by end of month	
LAYA Ltd	£2000 invoice. Goods to be delivered on 14 April – terms cash on delivery	

4 Marks

Task 2 (10 Marks)

(a) ABC Ltd has the following bank statement and cashbook.

Bank Statement Central Bank of Nortonainia			
Date	Detail	Debit	Credit
01/03/2022	Bfwd	513	
01/03/2022	Invoice X867657		24
03/03/2022	Independent Mortgage	42	
03/03/2022	Craftyfox	95	
03/03/2022	Hydrobank	27	
03/03/2022	Invoice X924713		69
03/03/2022	Invoice X502625		94
04/03/2022	Invoice X735449		52
06/03/2022	New Age Credit Repair	24	
09/03/2022	urban cave	41	
11/03/2022	Invoice X284568		3
11/03/2022	Bank interest received		14
13/03/2022	Bank charges	83	

Cashbook

Date	Detail	Amount	Date	Detail	Amount
			01/03/22	bfwd	530
03/03/22	Invoice X924713	69	03/03/22	Craftyfox	95
04/03/22	Invoice X735449	52	03/03/22	Hydrobank	27
11/03/22	Invoice X284568	3	03/03/22	Independent Mortgage	42
17/03/22	Invoice X862244	34	06/03/22	New Age Credit Repair	24
19/03/22	Invoice X342036	56	19/03/22	Time Cop	28
03/03/22	Invoice X502625	94	19/03/22	Iron Forge Mining	26
31/03/22	cfwd	464			
	Total	772		Total	772

What is the balance on the cashbook at 31 March 2022 and 1 April 2022?

Balance at	Amount	Debit	Credit
31 March 2022 cfwd			
1 April 2022 bfwd			

8 Marks

(b) ABC Ltd is concerned about a purchase with a supplier who may become insolvent before supplying the goods. Which payment method would provide some insurance against non-delivery:

| Answer: | |

2 Marks

Options		
Faster payments	Cash	Direct Debit
Credit card	Supplier card	Bank draft
Cheque	BACS	Bank draft

Detail	Amount £
Invoice X967303	58
Invoice X967302	64

Determine any payments from the bank account that have not yet appeared on the bank statement (note marks are deducted for incorrect answers):

Detail	Amount £

3 Marks

Determine the bank balance at the following dates:

	Amount	Debit	Credit
Balance cfwd 31 March			
Balance bfwd 1 April			

4 Marks

Task 4 (10 Marks)

(a) Classify the following errors in XYZ Ltd's accounting system:

Error	Classification
Bank interest missing from the cashbook	
New office furniture included in maintenance account	
Purchase day book posted as Dr Trade Payables Control £1200 Cr VAT £200 Cr Purchases £1000	
Items purchased for cash entered as Dr Purchases £120 Cr Cash £120 Rather than Dr Purchases £210 Cr Cash £210	

4 Marks

Options		
Error of Principle	Reversal of Entries	Compensating Errors
Error of Commission	Error of Omission	Error of Original Entry

(b) ABC Ltd has posted two journals in error (there is no VAT)

	Dr	Cr
Journal 1	Missing	Sales £1,000
Journal 2	Purchases £3,000	Trade Payables £300

What amount will be in the suspense account before these journals are corrected?

	Dr	Cr
Suspense		

2 Marks

The total of debits in the trial balance is £150,000 before the suspense account is created. What is the total of debits and credits before the suspense account is created?

	Dr	Cr
Total of trial balance		

2 Marks

Which of the following errors (if any) would lead to the creation of a suspense account?

Error	Would lead to suspense account	Would not lead to suspense account
An error of principle posting motor vehicle expenses to motor vehicle at cost		
An error omitting bank loan interest from the cashbook		

2 Marks

Task 5 (10 Marks)

(a) XYZ Ltd has the following payroll expenses for April.

	£
Gross pay	80,808
Trade Union Contributions	727
Other employee contributions	484
Employers Pension contribution	2,424
Employees Pension Contribution	6,464
Income tax	15,353
Employees National Insurance	3,232
Employers National Insurance	1,616

What is the total gross salaries for April for employees:

	Amount (£'s)
Gross Wages	

2 Marks

What is the journal to the Wages Control for payment of net wages:

Detail	Debit	Credit
Options		
Options		

3 Marks

(b) ABC PLC has the following wages expenses for December

	£
Net Wages	57,236
Employers National Insurance	2,666
Employees National Insurance	1,777
Trade Union Contributions	266
Other employee contributions	266
Income tax	22,217
Employees Pension Contribution	7,109
Employers Pension contribution	7,998

Prepare the Wages Control Account

Wages Control

Dr	£	Cr	£
Bank	57,236	Wages Expense	88,871
HMRC control account	26,660	Wages Expense (Employer's NI)	2,666
Pension control account	15,107	Wages Expense (Employer's Pension)	7,998
Trade union control account	266		
Other employee contribution control account	266		
Total	**99,535**	**Total**	**99,535**

5 Marks

Options

HMRC control account	Other employee contribution control account
Pension control account	Wages Expense
Trade union control account	Bank
Wages Control	

Task 6 (10 Marks)

On 31 January a partially prepared trial balance had debit balances totalling £124,823 and credit balances totalling £122,853

The accounts below have not yet been entered into the trial balance. Complete the table below to show whether each balance will be a debit or a credit entry in the trial balance.

	Amount	Debit	Credit
VAT control account (owed to HMRC)	12,103		
Bank account overdraft	17,059		
Share capital	12,020		
Trade receivables control	15,172		

The totals of debits and credits in the completed trial balance are

	Debit	Credit
Totals		

4 Marks

Following review it is noted that the month's entries from the Sales daybook have not been posted to the account being

	Total	Net	VAT
Sales Daybook Totals	43,434	36,195	7,239

Update the trial balance following correction of this error

	Debit	Credit
Other accounts		
VAT control account (owed to HMRC)		
Bank account overdraft		
Trade receivables control		
Sales		
Share capital		
Total		

6 Marks

Task 7 (10 Marks)

ABC Ltd has the following entries for VAT from its daybooks in its control account. Which side of the VAT control account will the entries be posted?

	Amount	Debit	Credit
VAT on cash purchases in cashbook	1883		
VAT on cash sales in the cashbook	1812		
HMRC entry in Debit side of cashbook	1867		
VAT in the discounts received daybook	50		
VAT in the sales returns daybook	49		
VAT on cash sales in the petty cashbook	74		

6 Marks

The balance bfwd on the VAT control account is set out below. What is the balance carried forward after posting the above to the control account?

	Debit	Credit
Balance bfwd		429
Balance cfwd		

4 Marks

Task 8 (10 Marks)

The following accounts have been extracted from the Purchase ledger for ABC Ltd

James Ltd
| | b/d | 3,027 |

Jim Ltd
| | b/d | 3,460 |

Jimmy Limited
| | b/d | 3,296 |

Jack Ltd
| b/d | 3,981 | |

The following balances have been extracted from the general ledger.

	Debit	Credit
Trade receivables control account	6,480	
Trade payables control account		6,480

Determine the difference between the Purchase Ledger and relevant control account

	Debit	Credit
Total of purchase ledger		
Total of Trade Payables Control Account		
Difference		

4 Marks

Which of the following errors is responsible for the failure to reconcile the control account?

Posting an invoice incorrectly twice to the purchase ledger for £678	
Posting an invoice incorrectly twice to the purchase ledger for £7284	
Posting a discount received incorrectly twice to the purchase ledger for £7284	
Posting a discount received incorrectly twice to the purchase ledger for £678	

6 Marks

Task 9 (10 Marks)

(a) The following transactions occurred in January. Record the transactions in the Trade Payables Control Account and show the balance carried down.

Balance bfwd (credit balance)	11239
Purchases	12799
Purchases returns	1667
Discounts received	1943
Payments	16950

Trade Payables Control Account

Options		Options	
Options		Options	
Options		Options	
Options		Options	
Total		Total	

Options

Purchase returns	Payments	Balance bfwd
Discounts received	Balance cfwd	Purchases

6 Marks

(b) In which daybook are the following transactions recorded:

Transaction	Daybook
Updating the general ledger account for interest received in the bank statement but not in the general ledger	
Correcting a purchase invoice posted twice to the Trade Payables Control account in error – all other entries being correct	
VAT in the Sales Daybook not correctly totaled and being posted in error to the VAT control account – all other entries being correct	
Posting small expense claims paid in physical cash to staff	

4 Marks

Options

Sales daybook	Purchases daybook	Cashbook
The Journal	Petty cashbook	Discount received daybook

Task 10 (10 Marks)

Jim Janey is opening up his own business. He brings the following assets into the business at the start of trading.

Item	Value (£'s)
A computer	769
Bank account	1593
Kettle, microwave and fridge	169
Amounts owed to suppliers	643
A car	7890
Amounts owed by customers	1061
Credit card debts for purchases	570

(a) Complete the opening journal for the business

	Debit	Credit
A computer		
Bank account		
Kettle, microwave and fridge		
Trade payables		
A car		
Trade receivables		
Credit card debts for purchases		
Shareholder funds		
Total		

5 Marks

(b) ABC Ltd has an irrecoverable debt as set out below. VAT was payable on the invoice at 20%

Amount excluding VAT	390

Update the balances in the general ledger following the irrecoverable debt transaction

	Amount before transaction	Debit	Credit
Trade Payables Control Account	18189		
Trade Receivables Control Account	45474		
VAT Control Account (amount owed to HMRC)	571		
Irrecoverable debt expense	201		
Sales	92676		
Sales Returns	2596		

5 Marks

Answers Task 1 (10 Marks)

(a) Match the payment method to the situation

Situation	Answer
Payment sent through post	Cheque
Reimbursement of small expenses for a meeting	Cash
Variable payment at the end of each month for electricity	Direct Debit
Fuel expenses for a fleet of vehicles all using the same franchise of garages	Supplier card

4 Marks

(b)

Debit card purchase	**Supplier card**	Faster Payments	BACS	**Cheque**

2 Marks

(c)

ABC Ltd	£2000 invoice dated 12 April 2022 – terms net monthly	4
XYZ plc	£2000 invoice dated 12 April 2022 – terms 2% discount if paid within 7 days, payment due within 14 days	2
OBO LLP	£2000 invoice dated 12 April 2022 – terms payment by end of month	3
LAYA Ltd	£2000 invoice. Goods to be delivered on 14 April – terms cash on delivery	1

4 Marks

Task 2 (10 Marks)

(a) For any bank reconciliation question you must always complete the full bank reconciliation. This will provide 100% guarantee of knowing if your answer is correct.

Previous months bank reconciliation

Balance per bank statement		-513
Add outstanding lodgements		
Invoice X867657	24	
Total		24
Less unpresented cheques		
urban cave	-41	
		-41
Balance per cashbook		-530

Updated Cashbook

				bfwd	464
11/03/22	Bank interest received	14	13/03/22	Bank charges	83
31/03/22	Cfwd	533			
	Total	1319		Total	1319
			01/04/22	bfwd	533

Bank Reconciliation

Balance per bank statement		-569
Add outstanding lodgements		
Invoice X862244	34	
Invoice X342036	56	
Total		90
Less unpresented cheques		
Time Cop	-28	
Iron Forge Mining	-26	
		-54
Balance per cashbook		-533

8 Marks

(b) Answer:	Credit card

2 Marks

Task 3 (10 Marks)

These are items that have already been posted to the cashbook and were not in the bank statement at the end of last month.

Previous months bank reconciliation

Balance per bank statement		-133
Add outstanding lodgements		
Invoice X967297	48	
Total		48
Less unpresented cheques		
Fourth Lookout Place	-79	
		-79
Balance per cashbook		-164

(c) Answer to part C Updated cashbook. These are the updated bank balances:

	Total	392		Total		392
	bfwd			bfwd		44
03/03/22	Invoice X967304	76	15/03/22	Loan interest		78
31/03/22	Cfwd	46				
	Total	514		Total		514
			01/04/22	bfwd		46

Bank Reconciliation

Balance per bank statement		-65
Add outstanding lodgements		
Invoice X967303	58	
Invoice X967302	64	
Total		122
Less unpresented cheques		
Gold Dreams	-69	
Glass Total	-34	
Total		-103
Balance per cashbook		-46

Detail	Amount £
Invoice X967303	58
Invoice X967302	64
0 marks if there is another entry	

3 Marks

Detail	Amount

	£
Gold Dreams	69
Glass Total	34
0 marks if there is another entry	

3 Marks

Task 4 (10 Marks)

(a) Classify the following errors in XYZ Ltd's accounting system:

Error	Classification
Bank interest missing from the cashbook	Error of Omission
New office furniture included in maintenance account	Error of Principle
Purchase day book posted as Dr Trade Payables Control £1200 Cr VAT £200 Cr Purchases £1000	Reversal of Entries
Items purchased for cash entered as Dr Purchases £120 Cr Cash £120 Rather than Dr Purchases £210 Cr Cash £210	Error of Original Entry

4 Marks

(b)

	Dr	Cr
Suspense		£1,700

2 Marks

	Dr	Cr
Total of trial balance	£150,000	£148,300

2 Marks

Error	Would lead to suspense account	Would not lead to suspense account
An error of principle posting motor vehicle expenses to motor vehicle at cost		Would not lead to suspense account
An error omitting bank loan interest from the cashbook		Would not lead to suspense account

2 Marks

Task 5

(a) Total cost to the employer	84,848
Employers Pension contribution	2,424
Employers National Insurance	1,616
Gross pay	80,808
Income tax	15,353
Employees National Insurance	3,232
Employees Pension Contribution	6,464
Trade Union Contributions	727
Other employee contributions	484
Net Wages	54,548

			£	£
Dr	Wages Expense		84,848	
	Cr	Wages control account		84,848
Dr	Wages control account		20,201	
	Cr	HMRC control account		20,201
Dr	Wages control account		8,888	
	Cr	Pension control account		8,888
Dr	Wages control account		727	
	Cr	Trade union control account		727
Dr	Wages control account		484	
	Cr	Other employee contribution control account		484
Dr	Wages control account		54,548	
	Cr	Bank		54,548

Wages Control Account

HMRC control account	20,201	Wages Expense	84,848
Pension control account	8,888		
Trade union control account	727		
Other employee contribution control account	484		
Bank	54,548		
	84,848		84,848

Task 6 (10 Marks)

(a)

	Amount	Debit	Credit
VAT control account (owed to HMRC)	12,103		12,103
Bank account overdraft	17,059		17,059
Share capital	12,020	12,020	
Trade receivables control	15,172	15,172	

Note that the share capital is a debit because this is the difference between assests – liabilities – the provision of the amount with the idea that some would use deadclic to make it a credit was a trick.

The totals of debits and credits in the completed trial balance are

	Debit	Credit
Totals	152,015	152,015

4 Marks

(b) Update the trial balance following correction of this error

	Debit	Credit
Other accounts	124,823	122,853
VAT control account (owed to HMRC)		19,342
Bank account overdraft		17,059
Trade receivables control	58,606	
Sales		36,195
Share capital	12,020	
Total	195,449	195,449

Note that to complete this question you should use T accounts as the share capital account moves from a debit to a credit

6 Marks

Task 7 (10 Marks)

(a)

	Amount	Debit	Credit
VAT on cash purchases in cashbook	1883	1883	
VAT on cash sales in the cashbook	1812		1812
HMRC entry in Debit side of cashbook	1867		1867
VAT in the discounts received daybook	50		50
VAT in the sales returns daybook	49	49	
VAT on cash sales in the petty cashbook	74		74

6 Marks

(b)

	Debit	Credit
Balance bfwd		429
Balance cfwd	2300	

VAT Control Account

		b/d	429
VAT on cash purchases in cashbook	1883	VAT on cash sales in the cashbook	1812
VAT in the sales returns daybook	49	HMRC entry in Debit side of cashbook	1867
		VAT in the discounts received daybook	50
		VAT on cash sales in the petty cashbook	74
c/d	2300		
Total	4232	Total	4232

Task 8 (10 Marks)

(a)	Debit	Credit
Total of purchase ledger		5,802
Total of Trade Payables Control Account		6,480
Difference	678	

Impact of journal posted on purchase ledger	Debit	Credit	Purchase ledger when reversed
Posting an invoice incorrectly twice to the purchase ledger for £678		678	5,124
Posting an invoice incorrectly twice to the purchase ledger for £7284		7,284	-1,482
Posting a discount received incorrectly twice to the purchase ledger for £7284	7,284		13,086
Posting a discount received incorrectly twice to the purchase ledger for £678	678		6,480

Task 9 (10 Marks)

(a)

Trade Payables Control Account

Purchase returns	1667	Balance bfwd	11239
Discounts received	1943	Purchases	12799
Payments	16950		
Balance cfwd	3478		
Total	24038		24038

(b) Which daybook are the following transactions recorded:

Transaction	Daybook
Updating the general ledger account for interest received in the bank statement but not in the general ledger	Cashbook
Correcting a purchase invoice posted twice to the Trade Payables Control account in error – all other entries being correct	The Journal
VAT in the Sales Daybook not correctly totaled and being posted in error to the VAT control account – all other entries being correct	The Journal
Posting small expense claims paid in physical cash to staff	Petty Cashbook

Task 10 (10 Marks)

(a)

	Debit	Credit
A computer	769	
Bank account	1593	
Kettle, microwave and fridge	169	
Trade payables		643
A car	7890	
Trade receivables	1061	
Credit card debts for purchases		570
Shareholder funds		10269
Total	11482	11482

5 Marks

(b)
Note that the amount excludes VAT such that the irrecoverable expense is £390 VAT is on top and the gross was the debtor in the sales ledger.

	Amount before transaction	Debit	Credit
Trade Payables Control Account	18189		18189
Trade Receivables Control Account	45474	45006	
VAT Control Account (amount owed to HMRC)	571		493
Irrecoverable debt expense	201	591	
Sales	92676		92676
Sales Returns	2596	2596	

5 Marks

Printed in Great Britain
by Amazon